Tapestry
CATS
AND
DOGS

Tapestry
CATS
◆ AND ◆
DOGS

AMANDA DAVIDSON

David & Charles

A DAVID & CHARLES BOOK

A catalogue record for this book is available from the British Library.

ISBN 0 7153 0167 5

Typeset by Ace Filmsetting Ltd, Frome, Somerset
and printed in Great Britain by Butler & Tanner Ltd
for David & Charles
Brunel House   Newton Abbot   Devon

CONTENTS

◆ • ◆

INTRODUCTION 6

GALLÉ CATS 10

STAFFORDSHIRE DOGS 20

VICTORIAN PUPPIES AND KITTENS 36

KITTENS WITH FLOWERS 44

STUBBS DOG 50

THREE-LEGGED RACES 56

RECLINING CAT 62

BUCCANEER CAT 66

CAT AND DOG FACES 70

PENNY FARTHING CLOCK 74

MEDIEVAL RUNNING DOGS 78

WALKING THE DOG 82

MAURICE AND LULU 88

CREATIVE STITCHES 94

MATERIALS, EQUIPMENT AND TECHNIQUES 112

DESIGNING FOR YOURSELF 116

STITCHES 118

FINISHING THE PROJECTS 123

SUPPLIERS 127

ACKNOWLEDGEMENTS 127

INDEX 128

INTRODUCTION

◆ • ◆

The tapestries in this book started life as a spare-time pursuit. I stitched during evenings and weekends, while my days were spent writing and illustrating "Teddy" books. Ten years and 13 titles later, my sitting room was filled to capacity with cushions, footstools and framed pictures. A simple urge to try something different had led me to pick up a book on needlepoint stitches. With no formal training in needlework and therefore no preconceived ideas, I studied the photographs and working diagrams. They looked fascinating and most important, easy to follow. From that first glance, needlepoint tapestry has become a growing passion.

Itching to stitch, I worked straight onto a blank canvas in primary-coloured embroidery threads, book at hand. Initially too lazy and impatient to pre-plan my design carefully on paper, I looked to a familiar subject – my family pets of cats and dogs – with which to experiment. Since pets are rarely far from our everyday lives, we are all capable of making a rudimentary image of one or the other from our memory. There couldn't be a more appealing and versatile theme on which to start stitching and designing. So this book steadily evolved, and with each project worked, my enthusiasm grew. There was, and still is, always something new to try.

If you haven't already discovered your full potential with needle and canvas, or are a newcomer to needlepoint tapestry, then I sincerely hope that this book will in some small way help to inspire you and give you the pleasure of developing and unlocking possibly unknown skills. By following the work of designers and emulating their ideas and techniques, you are guaranteed hours of enthralment. Take just one step further and you could be producing designs of your very own. Needlepoint tapestry is a joy to work.

The popularity of canvas work, one of the oldest crafts in history, is beset by conflicting terminology. Some say "needlepoint", others prefer "tapestry" or "embroidery". In fact, all three are correct, depending how it is approached. The word needlepoint is reflective of the small, regular stitches still known to us today as tent stitch and cross stitch. It was used by the ancient Egyptians and the Romans. Surviving examples of pictures and wall hangings from the Middle Ages use a mixture of fine embroidery and simple counted stitches on coarse linen.

In succeeding centuries the craft changed form as different countries developed their own stitches, yarns and ultimate uses. In the sixteenth century, it was discovered that needlepoint could imitate the more expensive techniques of woven tapestry beautifully. The exotic rugs and furnishings of the East could be available to all. With the addition of beadwork, there is no doubt that needlepoint tapestry will continue to inspire us for generations to come.

USING THIS BOOK

The projects have all been transferred onto charts for you to work from. Using a chart is really quite straightforward, a matter of counting stitches and referring to colours. These coloured charts were hand-drawn on graph paper in crayon and great care has been taken to match the yarn colours used. Each square represents one stitch. However, if you are in doubt, always refer to the manufacturer's code numbers as listed.

Where I have felt it easier, line drawings are provided for you to trace and the colours are indicated in simple code. There are also complete lists of materials and full step-by-step instructions, together with a guide to the technicalities of needlepoint at the back. I hope that you will find this book both helpful and enjoyable.

GALLÉ
◆ CATS ◆

These unusual creatures were inspired by a pair of ceramic cats in the Brighton museum. The originals were produced in pairs by French Art Nouveau craftsman Emile Gallé in 1880 and beautifully hand-painted in enamels with a variety of colours and floral decorations all over their bodies. An ornamental brown hood frames a mischievous face comprising a Cheshire-cat grin, a simple heart-shaped nose and distinctive glass eyes. Most intriguing of all is the chain medallion that these cats wear so proudly, each depicting the head of a hapless dog.

The yellow and blue cats are based on the original ceramic pair. The pink one shows how you can experiment with the groups of flowers and background colour. Like the original models, only the yellow cat has its tail showing.

In order to capture the intricate detail of the flowers, while still being able to stitch the simple background relatively quickly, I chose random long stitch. It is easy to work and extremely versatile, helping to create just the right flow of movement.

SIZE 21in (54cm) high. 156 stitches wide at the base, 291 stitches high from base to ear tip.

MATERIALS

- *14 mesh double or single white canvas, 20 × 24in (51 × 61cm) minimum*
- *Light-coloured waterproof marking pen*
- *Size 20 tapestry needle*
- *Tapestry wools as listed on the chart*
- *20 × 24in (51 × 61cm) backing fabric (I have used cotton velvet to match each cat)*
- *20 × 24in (51 × 61cm) cotton lining fabric*
- *8in (20.5cm) zip fastener*
- *Polyester filling*

Each cat is worked in random long stitch.

1 All three cats will fit snugly onto a 24in (61cm) wide canvas with very little wastage, but it is important to draw in the outline shapes before you start to stitch. If you are a beginner, you might want to select a wider canvas. Prepare the canvas as instructed on page 114 and mount it in a working frame if desired.

2 Group your yarn colours together into yellows, browns, pinks, blues and greens. Working methodically from one group of colour to the next will greatly simplify what may at first appear to be a complicated design. Leave large areas (white/ecru, background body colour, beige border) until last.

3 Following the chart, start by working the face, head and paws including the hind legs, using the brown groups of colours plus black. Stitch the eyes in green and the inner ears, nose and cheeks in pink.

4 Work the ribbon around both foreleg ankles and down the neck and body in pink, and the gold chain medallion in yellow.

5 Then follow the chart to work the flowers, leaves and butterflies. Work the browns that delineate the tail of the yellow cat.

6 Work the background colours – yellow, pink or blue – and then complete all white/ecru areas of the face, neck and front paws. Finish with the surrounding beige border.

7 Neaten the back of the work before removing it from the frame. Block if necessary (see page 115) and make each cat into a shaped cushion, paying extra attention to turning ear and head shapes (see pages 124–26 for instructions).

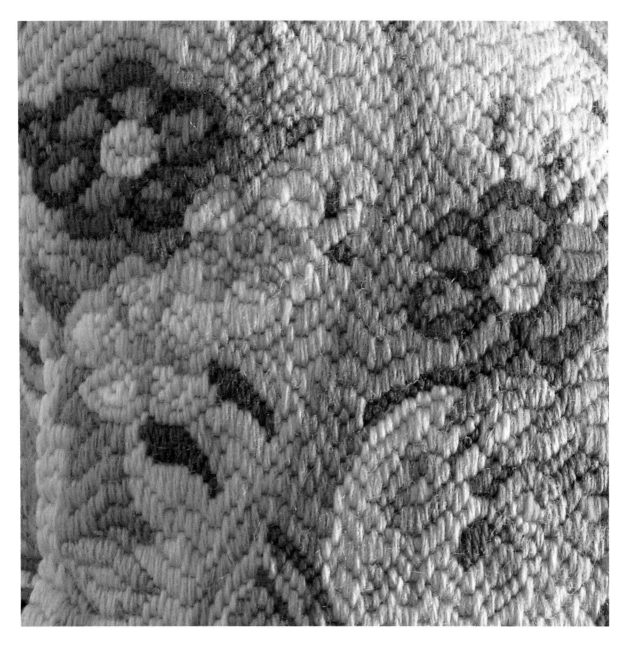

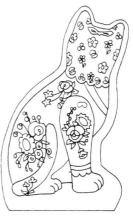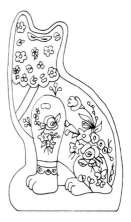

● Detail of pink Gallé cat (above)

If you are feeling adventurous, you could stitch the backs of the cats as well by reversing the outline of each chart. You can have fun restoring the blue and pink cats' tails to them, creating different flower designs, and decorating the back of the brown hoods that cover the cats' heads (see diagram).

● Rear view of the Gallé cats (right)

blue/pink Gallé cat　　　**yellow Gallé cat**

YELLOW GALLÉ CAT

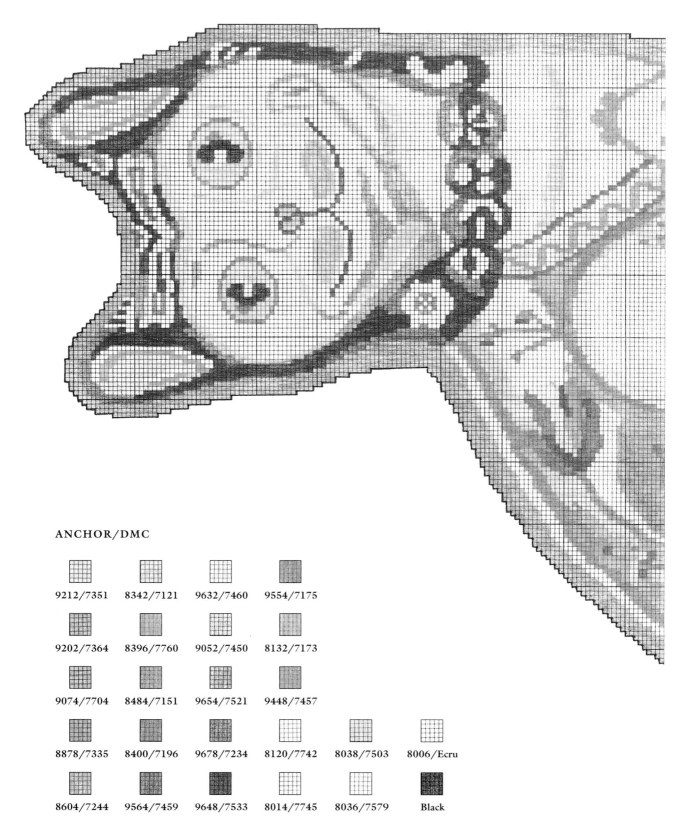

ANCHOR/DMC

9212/7351	8342/7121	9632/7460	9554/7175
9202/7364	8396/7760	9052/7450	8132/7173
9074/7704	8484/7151	9654/7521	9448/7457
8878/7335	8400/7196	9678/7234	8120/7742	8038/7503	8006/Ecru
8604/7244	9564/7459	9648/7533	8014/7745	8036/7579	Black

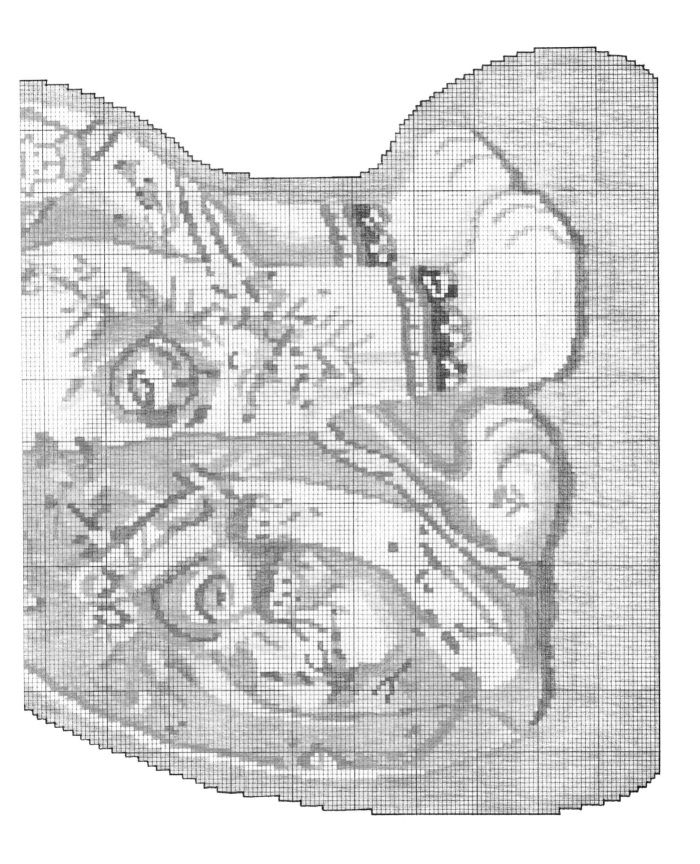

BLUE GALLÉ CAT

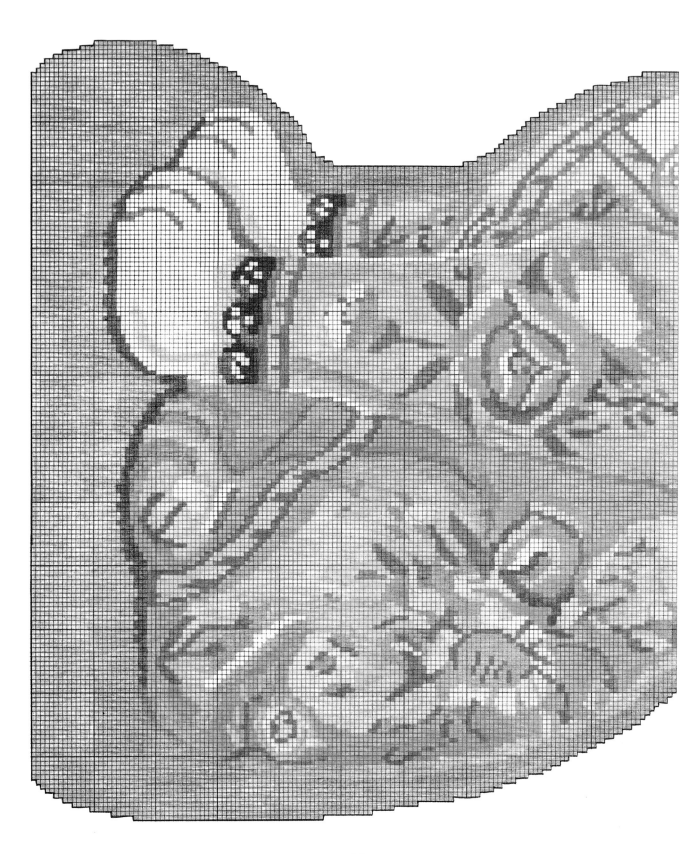

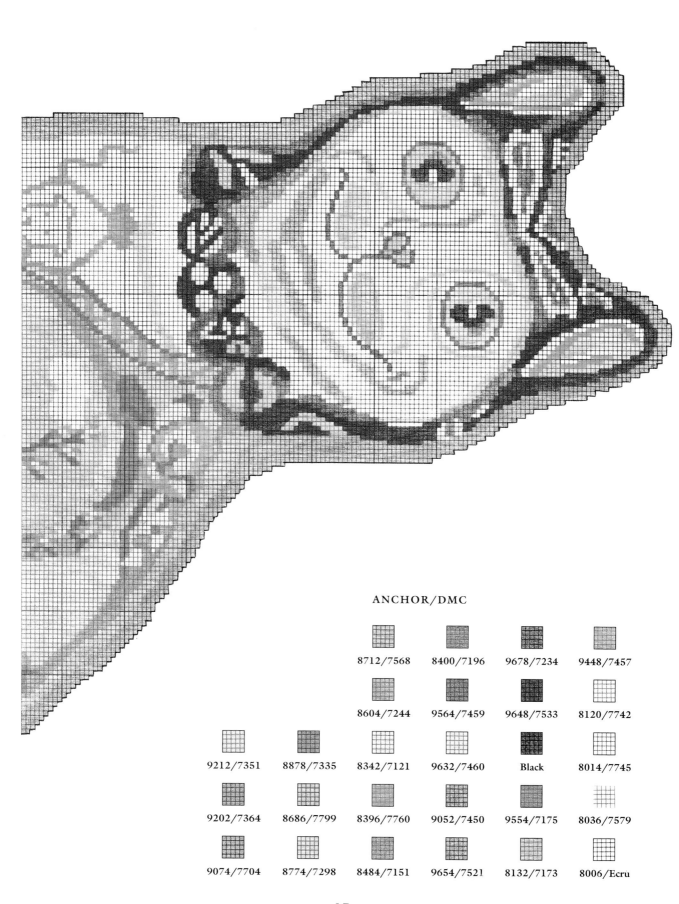

ANCHOR/DMC

8712/7568 8400/7196 9678/7234 9448/7457

8604/7244 9564/7459 9648/7533 8120/7742

9212/7351 8878/7335 8342/7121 9632/7460 Black 8014/7745

9202/7364 8686/7799 8396/7760 9052/7450 9554/7175 8036/7579

9074/7704 8774/7298 8484/7151 9654/7521 8132/7173 8006/Ecru

PINK GALLÉ CAT

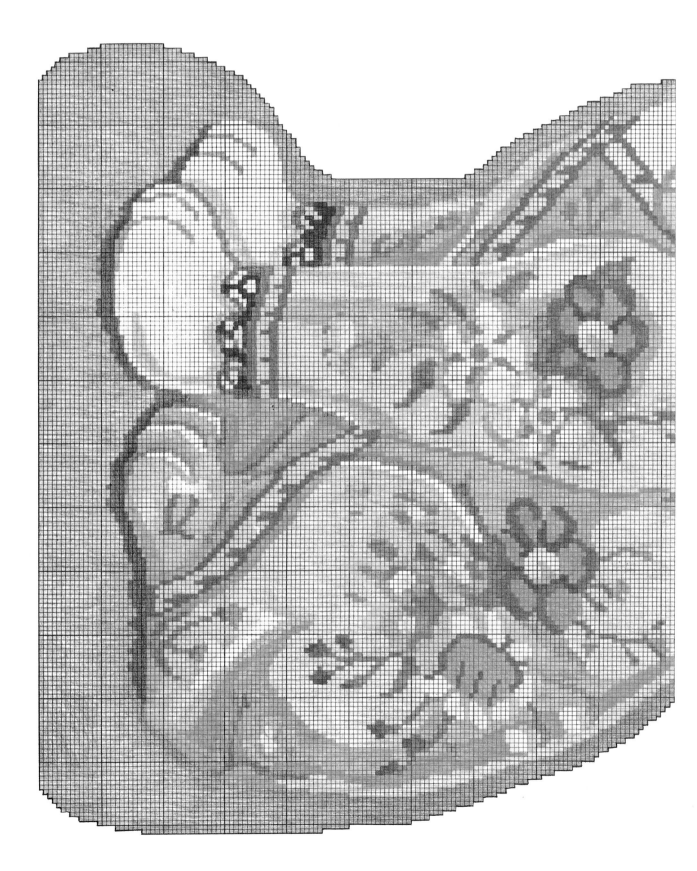

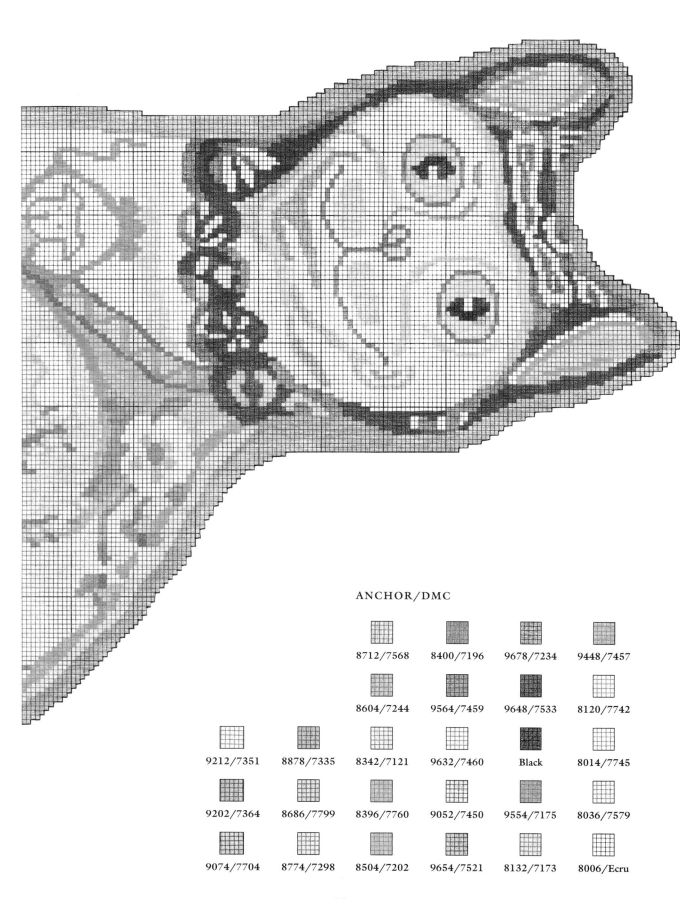

ANCHOR/DMC

8712/7568	8400/7196	9678/7234	9448/7457
8604/7244	9564/7459	9648/7533	8120/7742

9212/7351	8878/7335	8342/7121	9632/7460	Black	8014/7745
9202/7364	8686/7799	8396/7760	9052/7450	9554/7175	8036/7579
9074/7704	8774/7298	8504/7202	9654/7521	8132/7173	8006/Ecru

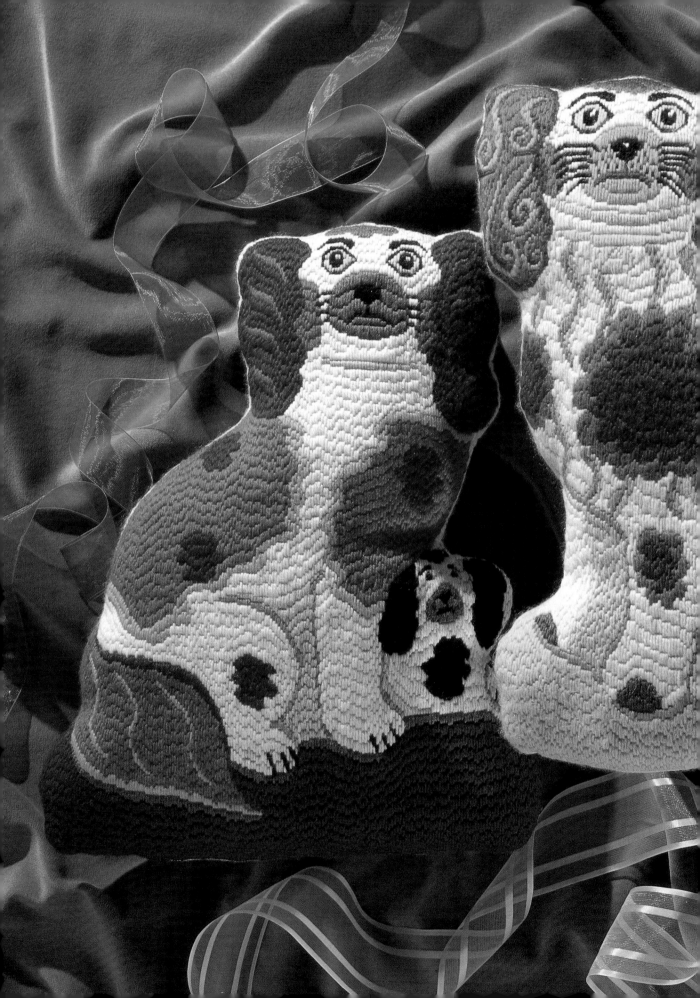

STAFFORDSHIRE
·◆· DOGS ·◆·

*Two dogs in an antique shop window in The Lanes in Brighton
looked on disdainfully as I sketched them. They obviously thought themselves exceedingly handsome
as they sat with languid yellow eyes and downturned mouths, like doggy
versions of the old English butler.
These Victorian chimney ornaments were originally created for the homes
of the "humble cottager" and designed for a mass market. The Staffordshire potters who made
them tried to imitate the appearance of expensive porcelain in their wares; the
press-moulded fur bodies were often simply painted or detailed with gilt stars or arrowheads.
Dogs were extremely popular subjects. Greyhounds, gun dogs, dalmatians, poodles
and especially spaniels sat or stood in pairs. Here are five examples based on authentic Staffordshire
designs to stitch. Reverse the charts to create a pair.*

*SIZES Black-and-white and Red-and-white: 17½in
(45cm) high. Dog with pup: 17in (43cm) high. Dog
with basket: 15in (38cm) high. Greyhound: 12¼in
(31.5cm) high.*

MATERIALS (for each dog)
- *14 mesh single or double white canvas, 19 × 24in
(49 × 61cm)*
- *Light-coloured waterproof marking pen*
- *Tapestry wools as listed on the chart*
- *Size 20 tapestry needle*
- *19 × 24in (49 × 61cm) backing fabric*
- *19 × 24in (49 × 61cm) cotton lining fabric*
- *8in (20.5cm) zip fastener (10in/25cm for greyhound)*
- *Polyester filling*

Each dog is worked in random long stitch.

1 Before starting to stitch, study each chart
carefully to familiarise yourself thoroughly
with the design. Each dog is different, and sits on
a different-coloured cushion of varying
proportions.

2 Using the light-coloured waterproof
marking pen, plot the outline shape of each
dog directly onto the canvas before you start to
stitch. *Black-and-white dog:* Count 241 threads
from the top of the head to the base and 168
threads along the bottom of the peach cushion.

Draw the outline shape, the position of the tail
and the curve of the back of the head. Next plot
the outline of each ear, then down the chest and
forelegs. Finally position his eyes, eyebrows and
snout with just a light dot on the canvas.
Red-and-white dog: Plot the outline as for the
black-and-white dog, counting 241 threads from
head to base and 166 threads along the bottom of
the yellow cushion.
Dog and pup: Decoration is kept to a minimum so
as not to distract from the adorable puppy. Count
236 threads from head to base, and 169 threads
along the bottom of the blue cushion. Plot the
outline as for the black-and-white dog, taking
extra care in positioning the pup. The faces are
deceptively simple but crucial to their charm, so
follow the design carefully.
Dog with basket: This dog, much smaller than the
others at 15in (38in) high, carries a cheery basket
of flowers in its mouth. Count 206 threads from
head to base and 134 threads along the bottom of
the pink cushion and plot the outline as for the
black-and-white dog.
Greyhound: Unlike the other Staffordshire dogs,
the greyhound, who lies with his forelegs crossed
elegantly in front and his head in profile, was
originally designed as a penholder for a lady's
desk. Count 168 threads from head to base and
243 threads along the bottom of the purple
cushion and plot the outline shape, the position of
the tail and the curve of the head as for the black-
and-white dog.

3 Prepare the canvas and mount it in a working frame if desired.

4 Don't be tempted to fill in the large simple areas yet; concentrate on the detailed parts of each design first, saving big areas and light colours until last. I like stitching the face first. Capturing the expression gives each dog its own particular character.

Stitch the outline of each eye in black, taking care to match both the size and shape, and ensuring that they are level. Fill in the black pupil and move on to the arched eyebrows. Bear in mind that each dog has its own individual pair. Take great care to finish off your ends neatly at the back of your work; black is notorious for showing through where it is not wanted.

5 Now follow the chart to complete the dog of your choice. Particular care must be taken when working curved shapes such as the curls on the tail and ears of the red-and-white dog and the dog with a basket, gradually increase or decrease by 1, 2 or 3 stitches at a time to create smoothly rounded shapes. Each flower on the cushion of the dog with a basket consists of a single yellow stitch over two threads with pink or blue petals stitched at random around it.

6 Finally, complete all large areas such as the dog's body and the cushion.

7 Neaten the back of your work and finish any loose ends before removing it from the frame. Turn to pages 124–26 for instructions for making shaped cushions.

RED-AND-WHITE DOG

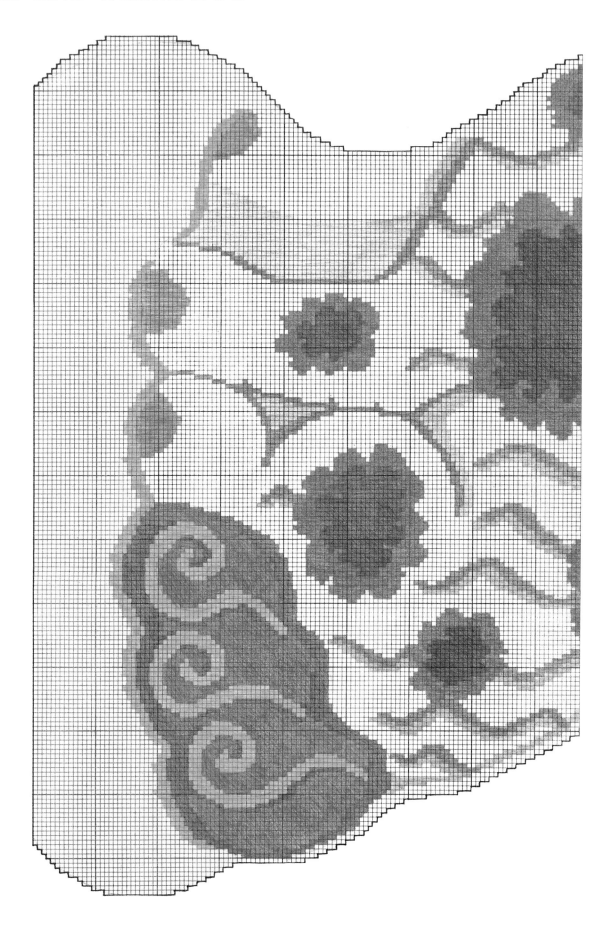

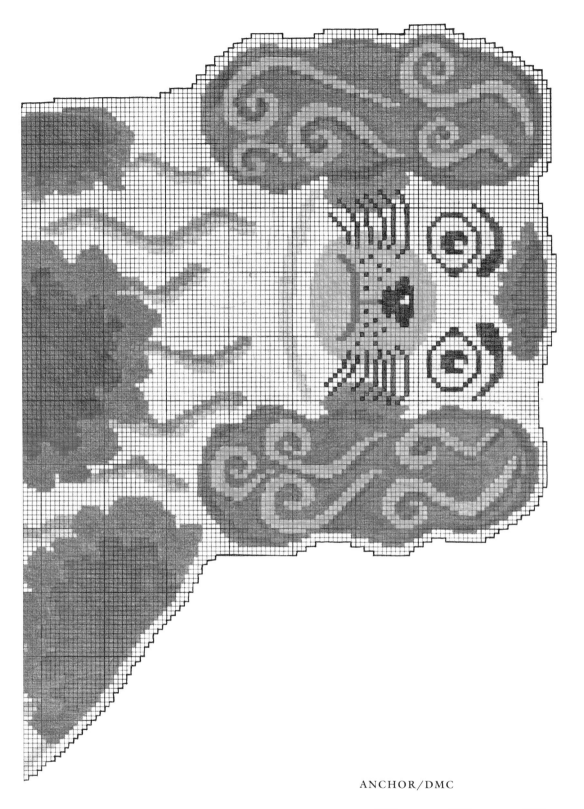

ANCHOR/DMC

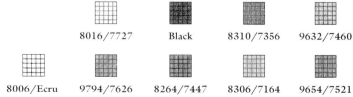

8016/7727	Black	8310/7356	9632/7460
8006/Ecru	9794/7626	8264/7447	8306/7164	9654/7521

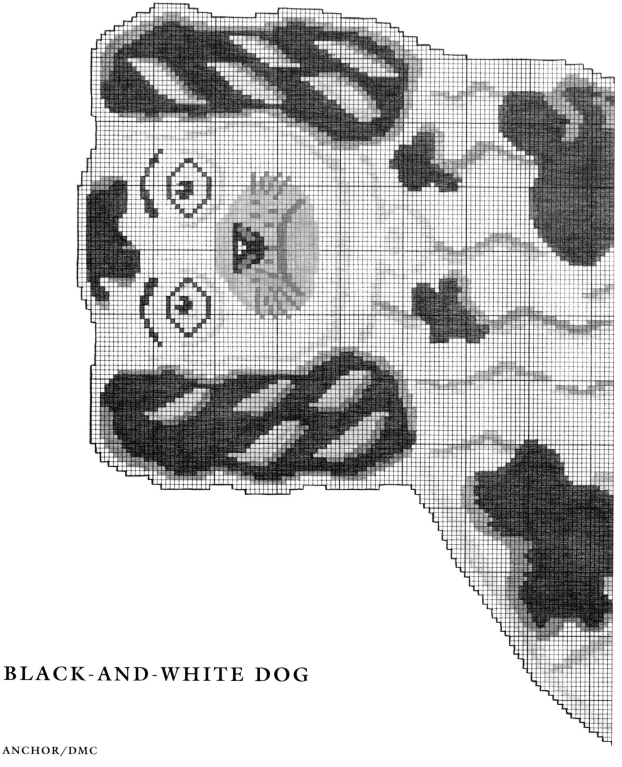

BLACK-AND-WHITE DOG

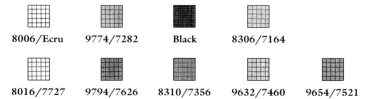

8006/Ecru   9774/7282   Black   8306/7164

8016/7727   9794/7626   8310/7356   9632/7460   9654/7521

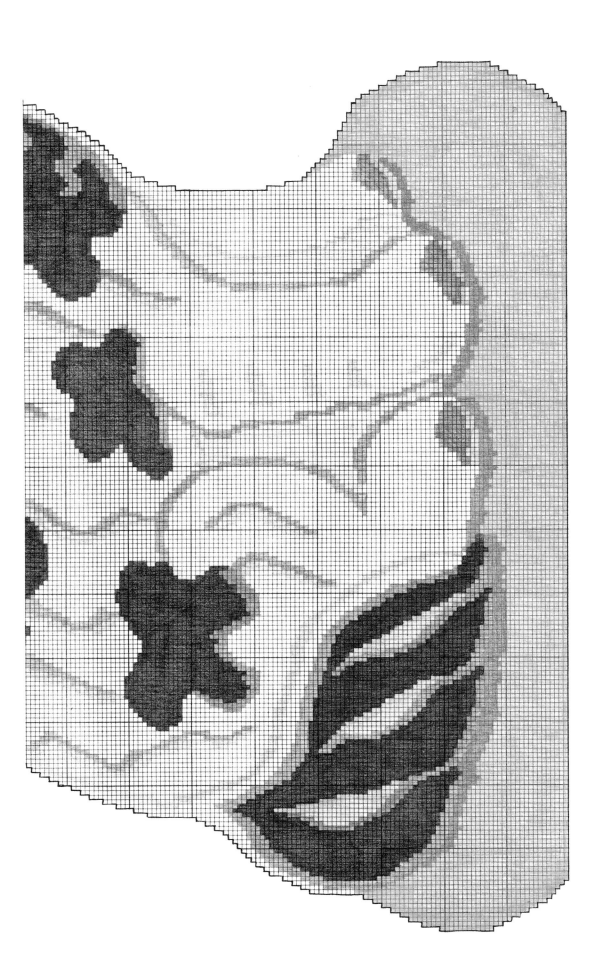

DOG WITH PUP

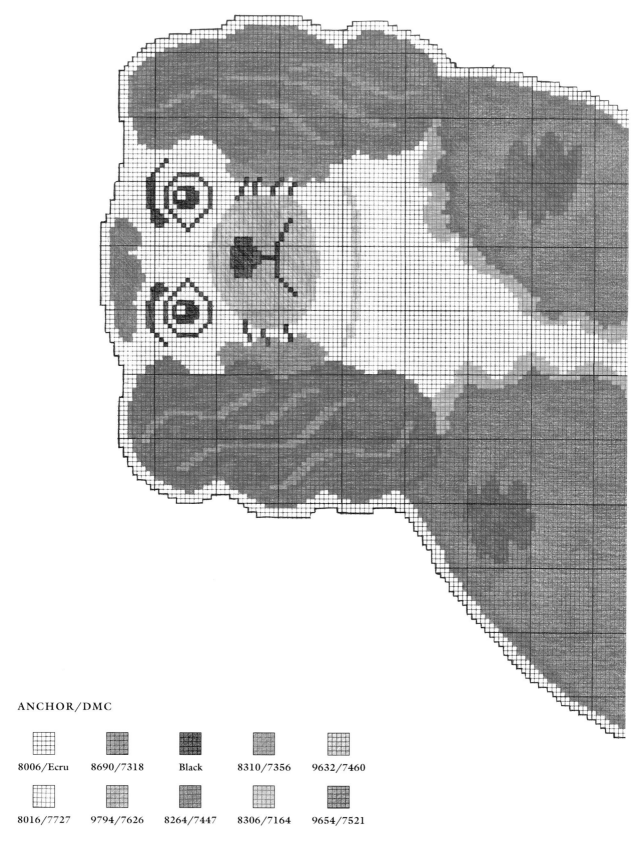

ANCHOR/DMC

8006/Ecru	8690/7318	Black	8310/7356	9632/7460
8016/7727	9794/7626	8264/7447	8306/7164	9654/7521

30

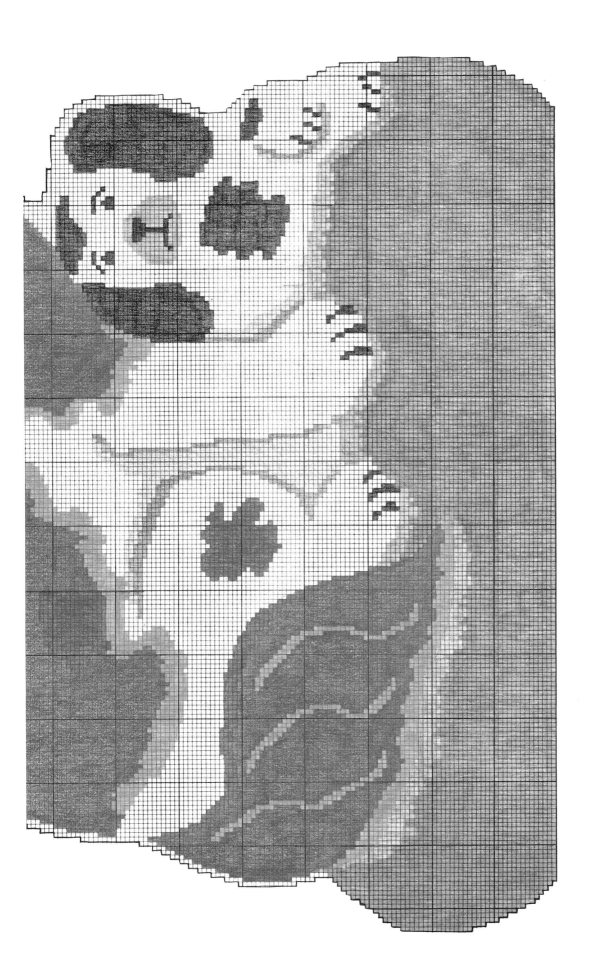

DOG WITH BASKET

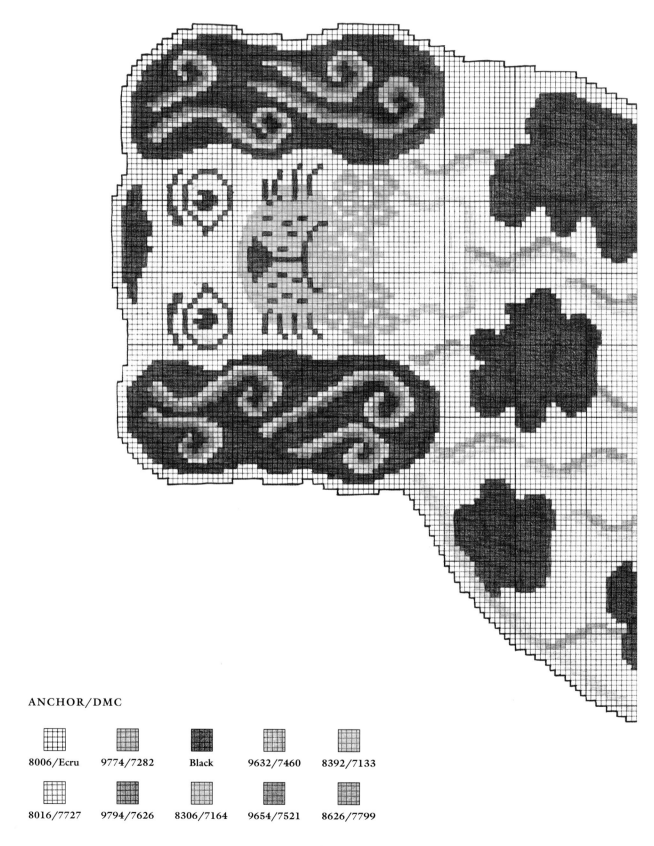

ANCHOR/DMC

8006/Ecru	9774/7282	Black	9632/7460	8392/7133
8016/7727	9794/7626	8306/7164	9654/7521	8626/7799

GREYHOUND

ANCHOR/DMC

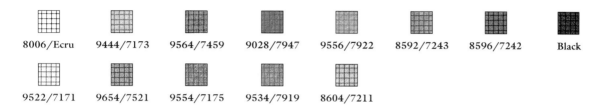

8006/Ecru	9444/7173	9564/7459	9028/7947	9556/7922	8592/7243	8596/7242	Black

9522/7171	9654/7521	9554/7175	9534/7919	8604/7211

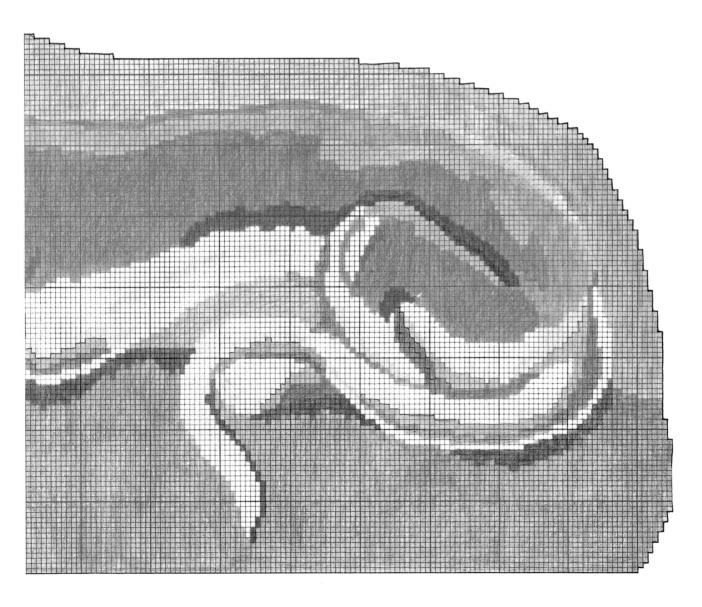

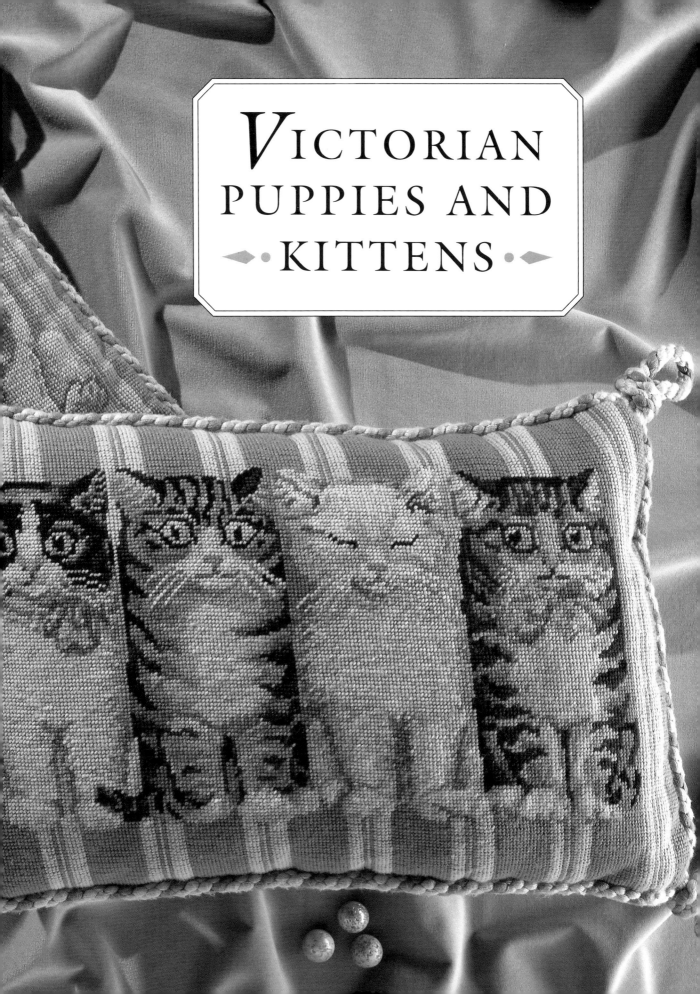

VICTORIAN PUPPIES AND ·◆· KITTENS ·◆·

The Victorians surrounded themselves with decorative images of their pets,
from moulded buttons and umbrella handles to painted china and greetings cards.
Commercial packing too reflected the craze, even if it was totally unconnected with the
product advertised. As attitudes towards the upbringing of children changed,
there was a growing emphasis on entertainment as well as instruction. Puppies and kittens
played their part as nursery companions in real life as well as in fiction. Newly
mass-produced books and toys portrayed both in a most sentimental way.
My two designs are typical of this exuberant style. These amusingly animated characters are
worked in warm, rich colours, though you may choose to alter the colour of the background
stripes to match your decor. I hope that you enjoy stitching them as much as I have.

SIZE (for each) 14½×22½in (37×57.5cm). 224
stitches wide×144 stitches deep.

MATERIALS (for each)
- *10 mesh single or double canvas in antique, 21×29in (53.5×74cm) minimum*
- *Light-coloured waterproof marking pen*
- *Ruler*
- *Size 18 tapestry needle*
- *Tapestry wool as listed on the charts*
- *19×27in (48.5×69cm) backing fabric (I have used cotton velvet to match darkest background wool colour)*
- *12in (31cm) zip fastener*
- *3yd (3m) matching braid*
- *Polyester filling*

Each design is worked in tent stitch.

1 Both charts are split exactly in half, with each half containing two puppies/kittens. Working in the same way for either design, lightly draw a dividing line down the centre of the canvas. Count 112 threads in each direction to give a total width of 224 threads. Count 144 threads for the depth. With the marking pen and ruler, draw the rectangular area to be worked. Prepare the canvas and mount it in a working frame if desired.

2 Use the background stripes as a guide to positioning the puppies/kittens. You may find it helpful to work part or even all of the background first. Starting with the darkest of the coloured stripes (at the top left-hand corner), stitch the top line only, changing colours as you work. Carefully count the number of stitches for each band of colour. When you are satisfied that the stripes fall correctly, either complete each stripe or merely stitch it in outline. You may find it easier to work the stripes that run behind the puppies/kittens by stitching the top parts down to the animals' heads, and work the bottom parts from the bottoms up.

3 You should now be left with each group of animals in outline. Using the colours as indicated on the chart key, begin by stitching one puppy/kitten at a time. Start with the head and work down. Don't be tempted to skip from one animal to the next. Working methodically will prevent mistakes from occurring!

4 Complete filling in the background stripes, if not already done.

5 Neaten the back of the work before removing it from the frame. Block if necessary. Turn to pages 124–26 for instructions on making cushions.

- *Detail from Victorian Puppies cushion*

VICTORIAN PUPPIES

ANCHOR/DMC

8006/Ecru   9502/7171   8366/7194

8398/7759   9448/7457   9552/7453   9324/7579   9656/7521   9662/7468

8442/7137   9564/7178   8060/7505   9388/7421   9678/7236   9666/7533

VICTORIAN
KITTENS

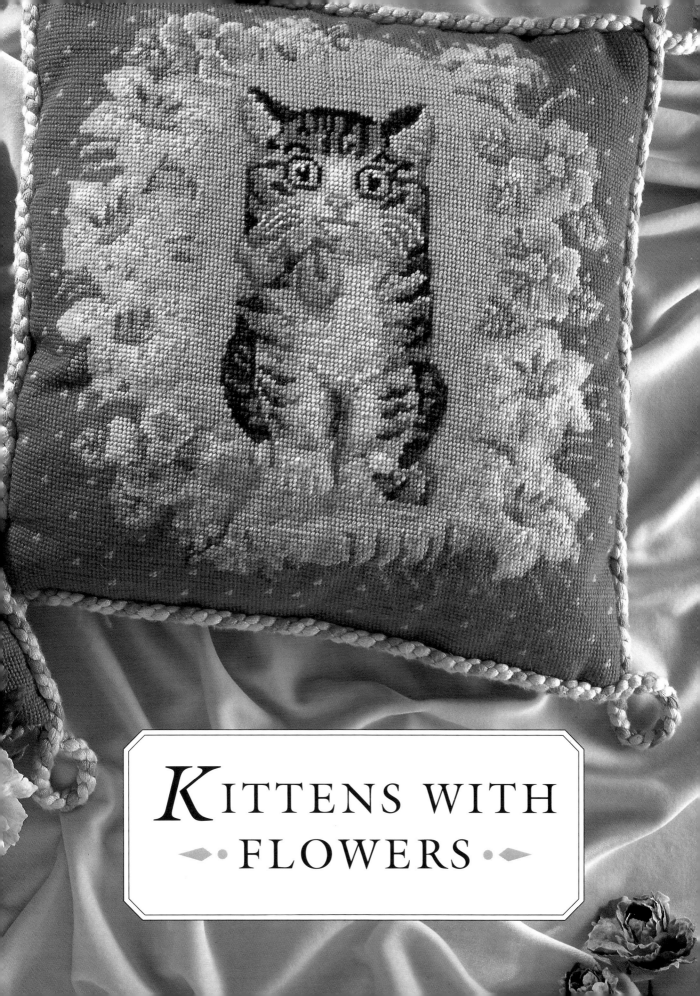

KITTENS WITH
◆ FLOWERS ◆

*C*ontinuing *the theme of Victorian kitsch, these two designs combine the two best-loved Victorian subjects: animals and flowers. The Victorians were also passionate about needlework, and girls as young as seven created highly accomplished samplers stitched on linen and using quite advanced techniques. The introduction of machines in the textile trade also meant that a wider variety of crafts became available.*

Most popular of all was Berlin woolwork, the forerunner of today's needlepoint kits. From Berlin came a range of richly coloured wool yarns and printed charts, to use with the new machine-made woven canvases, Berlin woolwork caught the Victorian imagination. The prolific number of examples that still exist are evidence of the boundless enthusiasm that marked the age. In each of these projects I have used traditional English cottage flowers with a kitten from my previous design. Try either of these designs with one of the other Victorian puppies or kittens on pages 36–43.

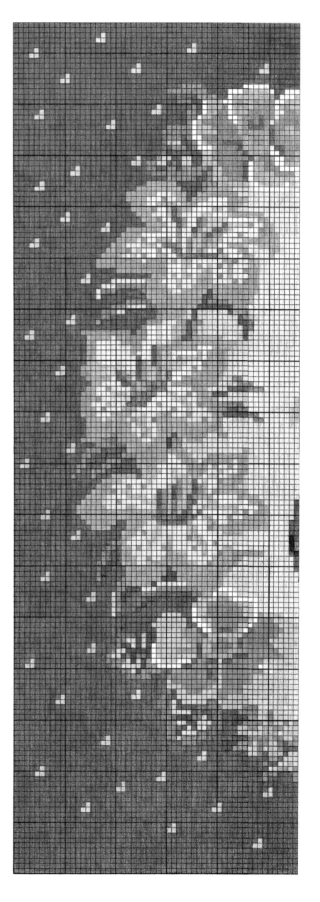

SIZE (for each) 16½×16½in (42×42cm). 166 stitches wide × 166 stitches deep.

MATERIALS (for each)
- *10 mesh single or double canvas in antique, 23×23in (59×59 cm) minimum*
- *Light-coloured waterproof marking pen*
- *Ruler*
- *Size 18 tapestry needle*
- *Tapestry wools as listed on the charts*
- *20×20in (51×51cm) backing fabric (I have used cotton velvet to match background wool colour)*
- *20×20in (51×51cm) cotton lining fabric*
- *10in (25.5cm) zip fastener*
- *2½yd (2.5m) matching braid*
- *Polyester filling or 16in (41cm) square cushion pad.*

Each design is worked in tent stitch.

KITTEN WITH LILIES

ANCHOR/DMC

8006/Ecru

9502/7171

8366/7194

8364/7192

8400/7196

8814/7301

8818/7302

8900/7690

9076/7394

9074/7704

9254/7371

9552/7453

9324/7579

9388/7421

9662/7468

9666/7535

1 There are two designs. In the first, a tabby cat is surrounded by a ring of peach-coloured lilies and pink and blue dog roses. The deep pink background is flecked with beige to add interest. The second design has a dark brown-and-white kitten circled by full-blown yellow, pink and blue roses. The brown ochre background is also randomly flecked with beige. I have exaggerated one or two of the colours on the charts to make it easier to follow. Working in the same way for either design, use the marker pen and ruler to draw the outline of the area to be stitched lightly on the canvas. Count 166 threads across and 166 threads down. Mark the centre point by counting 83 threads across and 83 threads down. Prepare the canvas and mount it in a working frame.

2 Approach whichever design you decide to stitch in the same manner: start by stitching the kitten first. You can either begin at the centre point by working the coloured ribbon and then the face and body, or start from the centre of the top line, counting down to the crown of the head, and stitch from the ears down. Either way, pay attention to the eyes, nose and mouth to capture the expression.

3 Next stitch the flower garland. Start from the centre of the top line and count down until you reach the first flower or leaf tip. Work methodically from one flower and leaf group to the next until complete.

4 Stitch the beige flecks at random. Finish by stitching the beige background behind the kitten and finally the darker outside border.

5 Neaten the back of the work before removing it from the frame. Block if necessary and turn to pages 124–26 for instructions on making cushions.

KITTEN WITH ROSES

ANCHOR/DMC

8006/Ecru

9502/7171

8366/7194

8364/7192

8400/7196

8814/7301

8818/7302

8900/7690

9076/7394

9074/7704

9254/7371

8038/7503

9324/7579

9388/7421

9662/7468

9666/7535

STUBBS DOG

George Stubbs was a master of painting animals. Better known for his horses, he also produced a splendid series of dog portraits. Never sentimental, his work reveals his understanding of anatomy. My attempt to capture the majestic quality of this pointer dog using rich brown and green wools instead of oils on canvas has been extremely satisfying.

Adapting the paintings of the old masters into needlepoint is not a new idea. However, it is a wonderful way of collecting your own artists' gallery of originals! The key to embarking on such a project is to use plenty of colour. Subtle changes in wool tints and tones will bring life to your work. A close inspection of any painting in an art museum will reveal how every brush stroke means something to the overall effect. Just imagine, you could do the same with every stab of your tapestry needle!

SIZE 16×23½in (41×60cm). 236 stitches wide×160 stitches deep.

MATERIALS

- *10 mesh single or double canvas in antique, 22×30in (56×76.5cm) minimum*
- *Light-coloured waterproof marking pen*
- *Ruler*
- *Size 18 tapestry needle*
- *Tapestry wools as listed on the chart*
- *16×23½in (41×60cm) footstool (for supplier see page 127)*

The design is worked in tent stitch.

1 The chart on pages 54–5 is split exactly in half. The 24 wool colours range from (1) off-white and cream to (2) light and dark browns and (3) greens and blues, some of which I have exaggerated on the chart to make it easier to follow. Sort the wools into these three groups before starting. Beginners may find it helpful to mark lightly with the waterproof pen when counting stitches.

2 Lightly draw a line down the centre of the canvas with the pen. Count 118 threads in each direction to give a total width of 236 threads, and count 160 threads down. With the ruler draw the rectangular area to be worked. Prepare the canvas and mount it in a working frame if desired.

3 From the base of the central line, count 58 threads up to the dog's stomach and mark this point lightly with the pen. Due to the tonal similarity of the lightest colours, I suggest you stitch the dark background areas around the dog's legs, head and tail first.

4 Stitch the head and dark brown patches on the body before tackling the whites and cream colours of the legs and stomach.

5 Finally stitch the line of trees and sky.

6 Neaten back of the work before removing it from the frame. Block if necessary. Turn to pages 124–26 for instructions on making a footstool or a cushion if preferred.

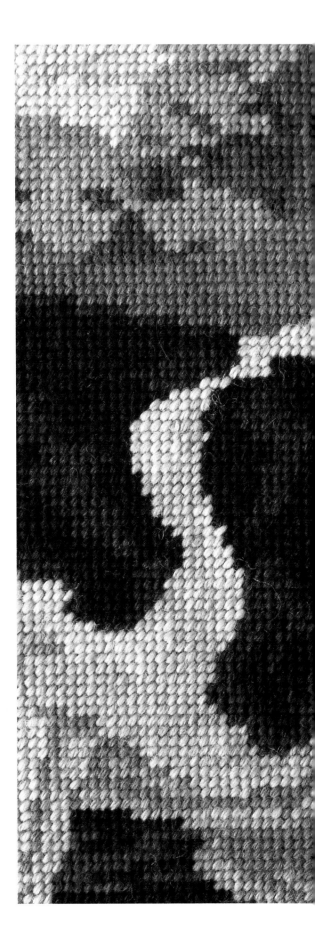

● *Detail of Stubbs dog footstool*

STUBBS
DOG

ANCHOR/DMC

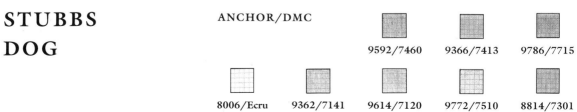

9592/7460   9366/7413   9786/7715

8006/Ecru   9362/7141   9614/7120   9772/7510   8814/7301

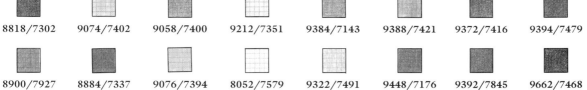

8818/7302   9074/7402   9058/7400   9212/7351   9384/7143   9388/7421   9372/7416   9394/7479

8900/7927   8884/7337   9076/7394   8052/7579   9322/7491   9448/7176   9392/7845   9662/7468

THREE-LEGGED
◆ RACES ◆

*T*he characters on these two cushions are
from a Victorian illustration, and they make me
smile whenever I look at them. Victorian
artists liked depicting cats and dogs wearing
human clothes for satirical magazines, annuals
and children's story books. Technological
advances in printing meant that coloured
illustrations no longer needed to be hand-painted.
The colours were dark and rich, using
mainly ochres, browns, deep reds, blues and
olive greens, and I have tried to capture
the look and feel of the era.
The "Three-Legged Race" cushion was the first
of these designs, and "The Wedding" was
a fun adaptation. By simply dressing the two
characters in different clothes and
altering the colours, you can create your own
personalised wedding gift – perhaps
matching the bride's dress.
There's no end to the possibilities.
It is also an amusing pun on the idea of
"Tying the Knot".

*SIZES The Three-Legged Race: 16 × 16½in
(41×42cm). 160 stitches wide × 163 stitches deep.
The Wedding: 16 × 16¾in (41×43cm). 160 stitches
wide × 166 stitches deep.*

MATERIALS (for each)

- *10 mesh single or double canvas in white or antique,
23 × 23in (59 × 59cm) minimum*
- *Light-coloured waterproof pen*
- *Ruler*
- *Tapestry wools as listed on the charts*
- *Size 18 tapestry needle*
- *20 × 20in (51 × 51cm) backing fabric*
- *20 × 20in (51 × 51cm) cotton lining fabric*
- *10in (25.5cm) zip fastener*
- *2⅔yd (2.5m) cord or braid*
- *Polyester filling or 16in (41cm) square cushion pad*

Each design is worked in tent stitch.

THREE-LEGGED RACE

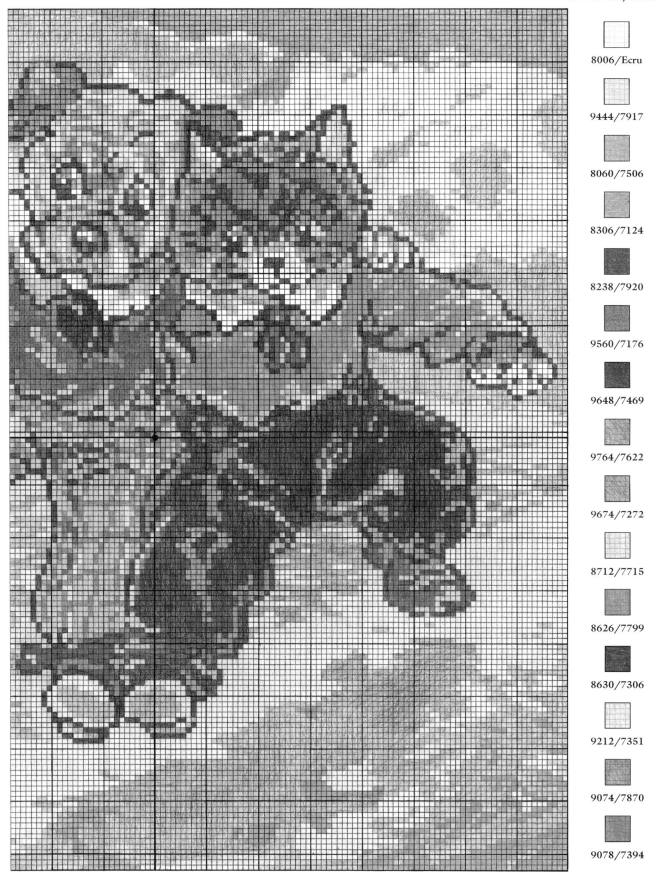

8006/Ecru

9444/7917

8060/7506

8306/7124

8238/7920

9560/7176

9648/7469

9764/7622

9674/7272

8712/7715

8626/7799

8630/7306

9212/7351

9074/7870

9078/7394

1 The working procedure is similar for both designs. Study the chart carefully. Each animal has a dark brown outline. I suggest you work this first, counting your stitches carefully as you work. Then fill in each area of clothing and body, leaving the background until last. Start by lightly drawing the area to be worked onto the canvas using the marking pen and ruler. Count 160 threads across and 163 or 166 threads down. Note that 'The Wedding' is slightly deeper to accommodate the dog's top hat. Mark the centre point by halving the width and the depth. Lightly draw a line down and across dividing the canvas into equal quarters. Prepare the canvas and mount it in a working frame if desired.

2 From the centre point, stitch the outline of the cat and dog. You will notice that the upper and lower half of each animal falls conveniently in one quarter of the canvas. Check the accuracy of your counted stitches regularly by referring back to the centre. When you are satisfied that it all looks correct, weave any stray ends of brown wool into the back of your work before proceeding to the next stage.

3 Now relax and enjoy filling in the clothing, faces, paws and feet. You need not count each stitch precisely, provided you follow the general shading for each garment and the fur markings. Minor details such as pink flecks on the wedding dress and veil can be worked at random.

4 Finally work the background, following the general patterns on the grass, footpath and the cloud formation in the sky, but again, don't worry too much about following the chart exactly.

5 Neaten the back of your work before removing it from the frame. Block if necessary and turn to pages 124–26 for instructions on making cushions.

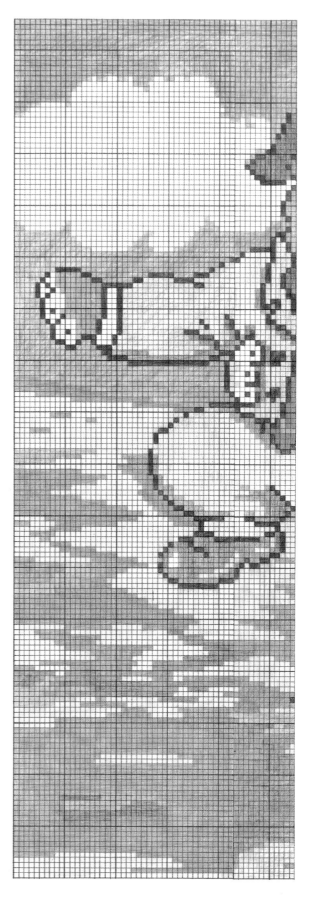

THE WEDDING

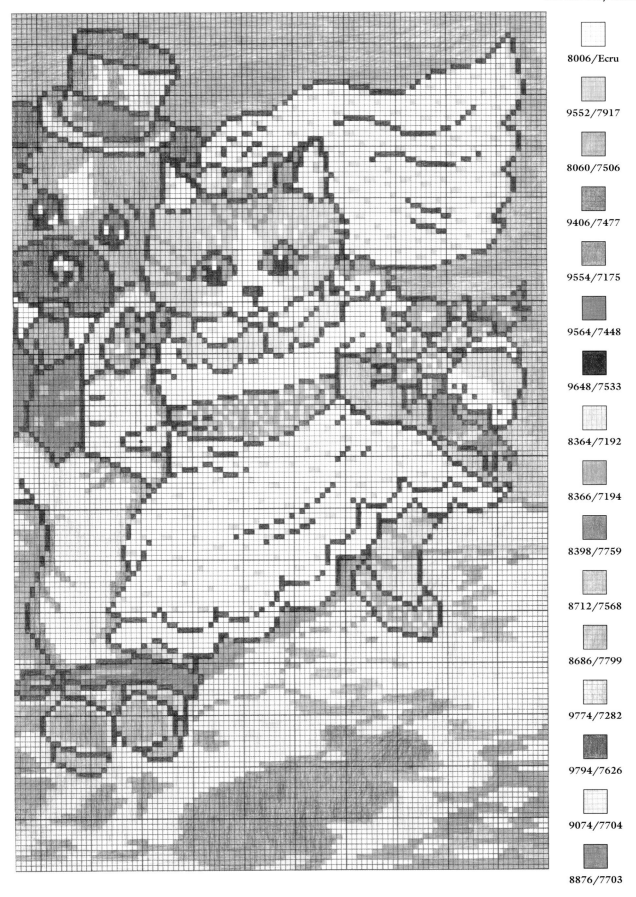

8006/Ecru

9552/7917

8060/7506

9406/7477

9554/7175

9564/7448

9648/7533

8364/7192

8366/7194

8398/7759

8712/7568

8686/7799

9774/7282

9794/7626

9074/7704

8876/7703

RECLINING CAT

*A footstool design that "worked" whichever way you viewed it had been
on my mind for some time. Creating a pattern with flowers posed little problem but
an animal, whether it is depicted standing, sitting, lying or running, will at some point be
upside-down. If it were round, I could have my animals running in circles.
This could work quite nicely, but would involve careful counting on graph paper to
make it look balanced if not symmetrical.
Feeling lazy and itching to stitch, the solution suddenly came to me. As my cat
Maurice yawned and stretched, he slowly rolled onto his back . . .
This design would also work as a cushion or could be made into a rug if it were scaled up
onto 7 mesh canvas and worked using two strands of tapestry wool.*

*SIZE 13in (33cm) diameter. 156 stitches wide × 156
stitches deep.*

MATERIALS

- *12 mesh single or double canvas in antique, 21 × 21in
(53.5 × 53.5cm) minimum*
- *Light-coloured waterproof marking pen*
- *Size 20 tapestry needle*
- *Tapestry wools as listed on the chart*
- *12/13in (31/33cm) diameter footstool (for supplier
see page 127)*

*The design is worked in tent stitch. Increase the back-
ground area for a larger footstool.*

1 Study the chart carefully. The black
background is marked with a dot for ease of
counting. I have exaggerated the greens and reds
on the chart to make it easier to follow.

2 Prepare the canvas and mark the centre with
the waterproof pen. Count 78 threads from
this centre point in each direction horizontally,
vertically and diagonally, marking with the pen
until you have plotted a circle. This method is
rather painstaking, but more accurate than using a

piece of string or drawing around a dinner plate.
Mount the canvas in a working frame if desired.

3 Following the chart, work the design from
the centre of the canvas outwards. Stitch the
cat, starting with the outline of his left paw and
leg. Follow the pattern of his fur until you reach
the head. The left eye is outlined in dark brown
and is located 28 stitches from the centre of the
canvas. Provided the cat's main features (eyes,
nose and ears) correspond with the chart, the fur
markings need not be as accurate. Complete the
head and work down towards the right foreleg.
Filling in the white/ecru areas at this stage may
help your cat take shape while you continue to
stitch the rest of the body. Some designers advise
that you leave all white areas until last in case it
gets dirty; personally, I rarely find this happens
unless you are stitching outdoors or with sticky
fingers, but it is a personal choice.

4 Once the cat has been completed, work each
group of the flowers and leaves that
surround him.

5 Finally stitch the black background. The
flecks of beige add interest and break up an
otherwise plain area.

6 Neaten the back of your work before removing it from the frame. Turn to pages 124–26 for instructions for mounting the work on a footstool or to make it into a round cushion. The black background will throw the other colours into strong relief, producing a striking effect. However, for a more subtle contrast, you may prefer to use a pastel tint such as sky blue, pale pink or even grey.

RECLINING CAT

ANCHOR/DMC

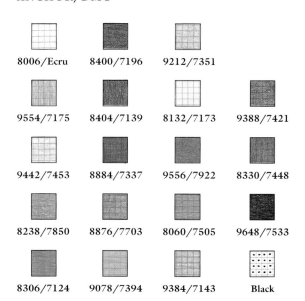

8006/Ecru	8400/7196	9212/7351
9554/7175	8404/7139	8132/7173	9388/7421
9442/7453	8884/7337	9556/7922	8330/7448
8238/7850	8876/7703	8060/7505	9648/7533
8306/7124	9078/7394	9384/7143	Black

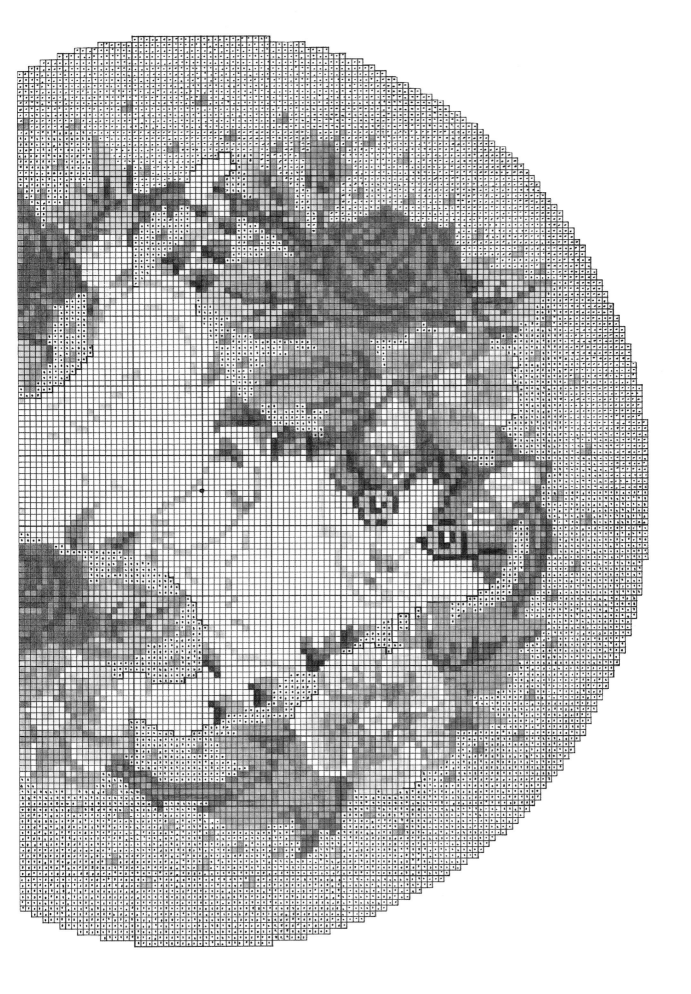

BUCCANEER CAT

This character is the Errol Flynn of the cat world, a swash-buckling adventurer with movie-star looks. Strong, brave and debonair, he is dressed to impress all the fair kittens and defend their honour against those dastardly dogs.
His elaborate costume of Spanish origin has a high ruff collar and bright red jacket with yellow brocade over a green shirt. His green hat sits jauntily over one ear and is trimmed with numerous plumes in yellow and peach. A bejewelled brooch on a deep green band and a skull and crossbones emblem complete the decoration.
Made into a circular cushion backed in plush velvet with a sumptuous border of tassels, the Buccaneer Cat will proudly adorn any room in the house.

SIZE 16in (41cm) diameter. 160 stitches wide × 160 stitches deep.

MATERIALS

- *10 mesh single or double canvas in antique, 24×24in (61×61cm) minimum*
- *Light-coloured waterproof marking pen*
- *Size 18 tapestry needle*
- *Tapestry wools as listed on the chart*
- *20×20in (51×51cm) backing fabric (I have used beige cotton velvet to match background wool colour)*
- *20×20in (51×51cm) cotton lining fabric*
- *10in (25.5cm) zip fastener*
- *1½yd (1.5m) matching braid or fringing*
- *Polyester filling or 16in (41cm) diameter round cushion pad*

The design is worked in tent stitch.

1 Study the chart carefully. A few colours have been exaggerated to make it easier to follow the chart, namely the pale green and light peach on the face, collar and hat plumes. His cheeks, chin and collar ruff, off-white in reality, are coloured pale pink on the chart. All the main details and markings on the cat's face are worked in dark brown.

2 Prepare your canvas and use the waterproof pen to mark the centre. Count 80 threads from this centre point in each direction horizontally, vertically and diagonally, marking with the pen until you have plotted a circle. Mount the canvas in a working frame if desired.

3 Following the chart, start stitching from the centre of the canvas using the dark brown wool. Work the left eye and stitch down towards the nose, mouth and chin. Then work back up to complete the right eye. Continue stitching all of the dark brown markings on the face and ear. You may also find it useful to stitch the dark brown of the hat band and brooch and the shadows under the collar ruff.

4 The next shade is brown ochre. Work all these patches on the face and ear, and on part of the collar ruff, the shadows, the left-hand side of the jacket and on the edge of the yellow brocade. Continue to work through the creams, beiges and white/ecru on the face.

5 Work the greens for the eyes, collar ruff, hat and some on the face.

6 Stitch the brighter colours on the jacket and hat plumes and the brooch.

7 Finally work the beige background and check that your design is nicely rounded.

8 It is very important to neaten the back of your work before removing it from the frame. To make the piece into a cushion turn to pages 124–26 for instructions.

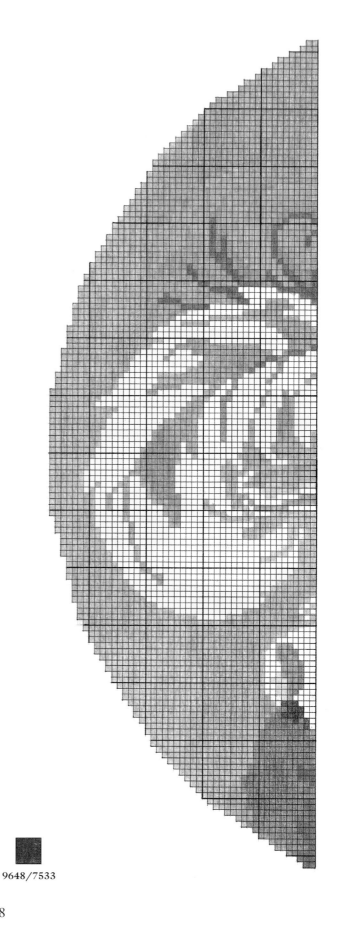

BUCCANEER CAT

ANCHOR/DMC

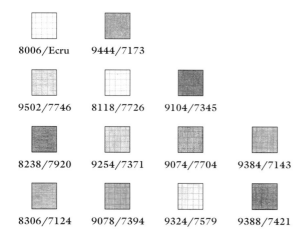

8006/Ecru   9444/7173

9502/7746   8118/7726   9104/7345

8238/7920   9254/7371   9074/7704   9384/7143

8306/7124   9078/7394   9324/7579   9388/7421   9648/7533

CAT
AND DOG
FACES

*T*he facial expressions of cats and dogs
are a vital part of their character. To capture this
liveliness within the confines of wool and canvas
is a challenge. The alteration of just one
stitch can make all the difference, as the sampler
in the photograph demonstrates.
Cats vary mainly in colour and length of coat
and so are easier to interpret. No domestic
animal is as varied in colour, coat, size
and behaviour as the dog, ranging from a tiny
chihuahua to a huge St Bernard.
The pincushion and waistcoat projects show what
can be achieved with a simple repeated
face pattern.

PINCUSHION

*SIZE 4in (10cm) diameter. 49 stitches wide × 49
stitches deep.*

MATERIALS

- *12 mesh single or double canvas in white or antique,
approximately 10 × 10in (25.5 × 25.5cm)*
- *Light-coloured waterproof marking pen*
- *Size 20 tapestry needle*
- *Tapestry wool as listed on the chart*
- *4in (10cm) diameter pincushion (for supplier see
page 127)*

This design is worked in tent stitch.

1 The chart opposite shows a repeat pattern of four dog faces against a tartan-plaid background. The centre of the design falls in the middle of a light pink downward stripe. Stitching this and the two corresponding horizontal stripes first will help to position the faces. Mark the centre of the canvas with the pen, then from this point count 24 threads across and 24 threads down in both directions, forming a cross, and mark it with the pen. Prepare the canvas and mount it in a working frame if desired.

2 Using the light pink wool, stitch the central stripes only. Next, stitch the dog faces,

positioning each one in relation to the stripes worked. When all four faces are complete, stitch the remaining light pink stripes.

3 Stitch the remaining background in deep pink, and finally the dogs' whiskers in black using straight stitch.

4 Neaten the back of your work before removing it from frame. Turn to pages 124–26 for instructions for making the pincushion. Try this project using a dog or cat of your own design. This could be an ideal opportunity to use the family pet as the model for your design.

WAISTCOAT

SIZE each front panel 4¾ × 8½in (12 × 22cm). 57 stitches wide × 101 stitches deep.

MATERIALS

- *12 mesh single or double canvas in white or antique, 17 × 15in (43 × 38cm) minimum for both panels*
- *Light-coloured waterproof marking pen*
- *Ruler*
- *Size 20 tapestry needle*
- *Tapestry wool as listed on the chart*
- *12 × 12in (31 × 31cm) backing fabric (I have used a dark blue moiré)*
- *Two 6½ × 10½in (17 × 27cm) lining fabric for front panels in matching blue*
- *Optional additions. Two gold decorative buttons approximately ½in (1cm) diameter. One length gold chain approximately 5in (13cm)*

This design is worked in tent stitch.

1 The chart opposite shows a repeat pattern of cat and dog faces against a light and dark blue striped background. This is the left side panel of the waistcoat. The right side panel is simply reversed. Draw a central dividing line down the width of the canvas with the pen. Working on the left side, plot the dimensions of the left panel. Count 57 threads across and 101 threads down. Mark the border lines on the canvas and join them

to form a rectangle. From the right of the base line, count 19 threads to the left and mark. Count another 4 threads and mark. This is the tip of the panel. A stitched combination of light blue stripes and faces will help you to be precise. Prepare the canvas and mount it in a working frame if desired.

2 From the tip of the panel, start by stitching the two light blue stripes. Using two separate lengths of wool, stitch first the right stripe (7 stitches) and then the left stripe (6 stitches). Leave the surplus lengths to the side. Now stitch the first cat's face. When it is finished, pick up the light blue wool and stitch the next two stripes as before. Continue in this way until the first line of cat faces is complete.

3 Stitch the proceeding lines of dog and cat faces in the same manner, remembering to keep the back of your work neat.

4 Stitch the darker blue background. Finally work the whiskers in straight stitch.

5 To work the right side panel, follow the above procedure, bearing in mind that the shape is in reverse. The faces remain the same.

6 Neaten the back of your work before removing it from the frame. Turn to pages 124–26 for instructions for making up.

PINCUSHION

ANCHOR/DMC

9322/7746 8400/7196 8396/7760 9662/7238

8404/7139 8310/7356 Black

WAISTCOAT

ANCHOR/DMC

8626/7283 9564/7459

8818/7304 9648/7533

9202/7364 9388/7513

8396/7760 9384/7143

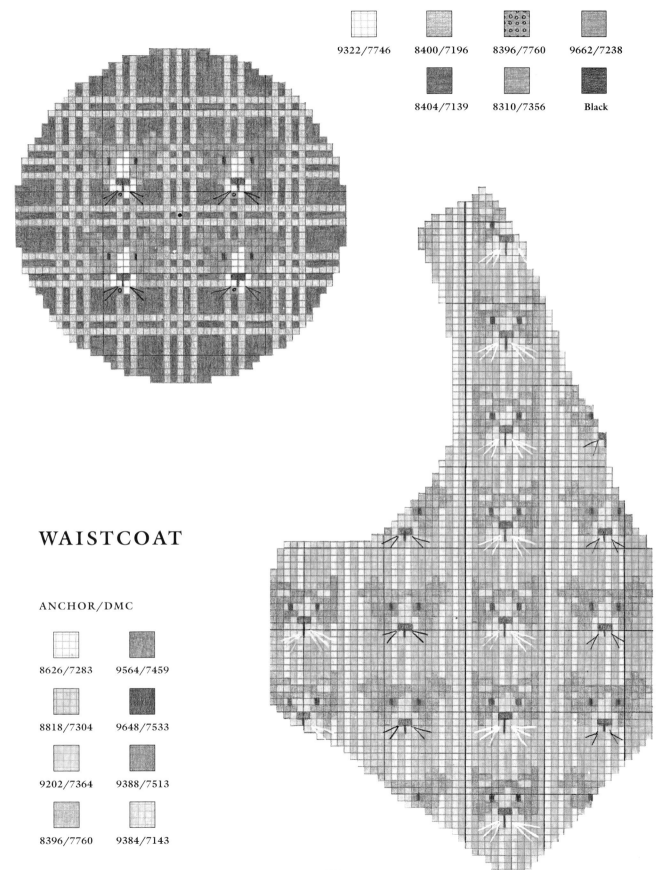

PENNY FARTHING CLOCK

If the likelihood of seeing a dog riding a Penny Farthing cycle seems absurd, imagine the reaction when the first man was seen on one in 1870. Sitting five feet off the ground on such an unstable contraption was extremely hazardous. Riders had to be highly athletic when mounting and dismounting. Brakes would not be invented for another 15 years, but this did not discourage the determined! The trick was for the rider to balance his (or her) weight toward the rear wheel. The rewards were magnificent views and speedy journeys, but unfortunately the uneven, stony roads of the day meant that rider and bike often "came a cropper".
It works much better as a clock design with the aid of a dog and a hidden battery.

SIZE 11 × 13½in (28 × 34cm). 151 stitches wide × 188 stitches deep.

MATERIALS

- *14 mesh double or single canvas in white, 17 × 20in (43 × 51cm) minimum*
- *Light-coloured waterproof marking pen*
- *Ruler*
- *Size 20 tapestry needle*
- *Tapestry wools as listed on the chart*
- *11 × 13½in (28 × 34.5cm) cardboard approximately ⅛in (3mm) thick*
- *Clock mechanism with hands not exceeding 3in (7.5cm) in length*
- *Cream cotton sewing thread and sharp needle*

The design is worked in random long stitch.

1 The chart on pages 76–7 is divided into two parts. You may find it helpful to divide your canvas into two as marked by the arrows on the chart. To draw the outline to the area to be worked using the marker pen and ruler, count 151 threads across and 188 threads down. Divide the depth by 86 threads from the top and 102 threads from the bottom. Some of the wool colours have been exaggerated on the chart, especially the light blues and creams. When stitching keep your tension fairly taut, especially around the clock face, as any loose stitches may impair movement of the hands. Prepare the canvas and mount it in a working frame if desired.

2 To work the clock face (the big wheel of the penny farthing), start from the left of the dividing line and count 71 threads across and 47 threads down to mark the centre of the big wheel. Draw a tiny square 3 threads by 3 threads around this point to form a block of 9 squares and leave this area unworked as this is where clock hands will be fitted after the design is complete. Using the brown wool, stitch the wheel spokes. Each spoke ends in a little yellow square which indicate the hours on the clock face. Using the same yellow, stitch the upright bar and pedals, then complete the pedals using the peach wool. Using the three greens, stitch the tyre. The inner rim is in the darkest green and the outer uses a combination of the remaining two shades. Stitch the small wheel in a similar way. Complete by

74

stitching the curved frame in the rust red and orange wools and the saddle in blue.

3 To work the dog, start with his pedalling legs in the off-white and pinkish-cream colours, working upwards. Stitch his front paws on the handlebars and progress to the darker shade of brown on his back, tail and head. Stitch the knapsack in the two lighter greens and turquoise, his collar in rust red, and finally his face, with its big peach tongue. Make your stitches resemble hair by following the shape of his limbs. The tail can be nice and shaggy, but keep the stitching simple around his jaw and muzzle. Never use more than 7 threads of canvas in a single long stitch. Neaten the ends as you work.

4 To work the background, stitch either the sky or land section first.
Complete by stitching the yellow border in straight stitch, horizontal for the sides and vertical for the top and bottom.

5 Neaten the back of your work. Finally, cut one vertical and one horizontal thread of the square that you left in the centre of the wheel. Pull back and secure neatly with small stitches using sharp needle and thread. If you are using double interlock canvas, you should be able to push the point of a pencil through the centre and gently ease the threads apart to create a nice neat hole. After you have neatened the back remove the work from the frame and turn to pages 124–26 for instructions for making the clock.

PENNY FARTHING CLOCK

ANCHOR/DMC

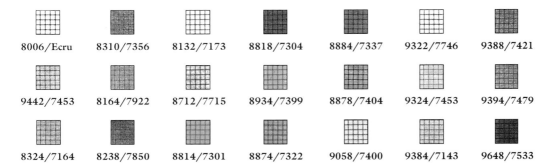

8006/Ecru	8310/7356	8132/7173	8818/7304	8884/7337	9322/7746	9388/7421
9442/7453	8164/7922	8712/7715	8934/7399	8878/7404	9324/7453	9394/7479
8324/7164	8238/7850	8814/7301	8874/7322	9058/7400	9384/7143	9648/7533

MEDIEVAL RUNNING DOGS

A detail of a seventeenth-century crewelwork bed hanging inspired me to create these two designs. Worked in long stitch, the pieces look medieval in style. Tapestries of this earlier period were often massed with detail and rich colour, olive greens and petrol blues strikingly contrasted by reds, browns and off-whites. Hunting was a favourite subject in which dogs played a major role. In search of the mythological unicorn, men and dogs scoured the countryside in action-packed scenes. This is my version of a detail from such a scene, made into a glasses case and trinket box lid.

SIZE (for each) 4½ × 8½in (11.5 × 22cm). 153 threads wide × 81 threads deep.

MATERIALS (for each)
- *18 mesh single white canvas, 10 × 14in (25.5 × 36cm) approximately*
- *Light-coloured waterproof marking pen*
- *Ruler*
- *Tapestry wools as listed on chart*
- *Size 20 tapestry needle*
- *Trinket box (for supplier see page 127)*

(For glasses case only)
- *6 × 10in (15.5 × 25.5cm) backing fabric (I used petrol blue cotton velvet.)*
- *10 × 10in (25.5 × 25.5cm) cotton lining fabric*
- *26in (66cm) length braid in gold.*

These two designs are worked in random long stitch.

1 Study the charts carefully. I have made them into simple line drawings so that all you need do is place your canvas directly on top and trace each design using the waterproof marker pen. Each number represents a wool colour. Where there are two numbers together, work each colour at random to create a mottled effect.

The length of each stitch helps delineate shape and form, particularly with the dogs. Make sure longer stitches are fairly taut and do not exceed 10 threads of the canvas.

Prepare the canvas and mount it in a working frame if desired.

2 Work the dogs first. Small details such as claws, eyes and nose are worked over 1 or 2 canvas threads.

3 Next work the background. On the chart I have simplified the clumps of flowers in the grass for ease of tracing. Make these as delicate as you like. On my finished pieces I have stitched groups of leaves in dark green over 1, 2 or 3 threads of canvas, topped by little white flower heads, but this can be varied as you wish.

4 The border on the trinket box design is a simple oval band in petrol blue. The same colour is used to form a rectangular border on the glasses case. Tiny specks of white stitched randomly over 1 thread of canvas add highlights.

5 Neaten the back of your work before removing it from the frame. Turn to page 126 for instructions for making the box top and the glasses case.

GLASSES CASE

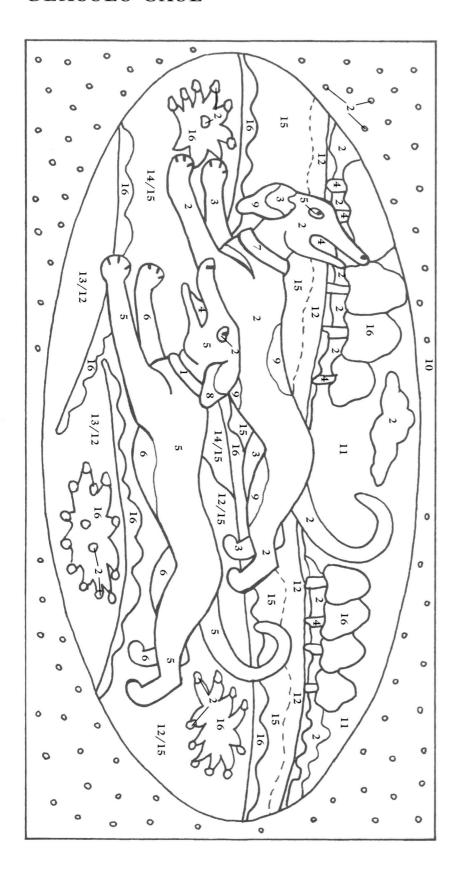

ANCHOR/DMC	
1	9648/7533
2	8006/Ecru
3	9614/7120
4	8364/7197
5	8310/7146
6	8262/7356
7	8238/7920
8	9564/7448
9	9388/7421
10	8820/7304
11	8874/7322
12	9212/7351
13	9174/7364
14	8878/7404
15	9058/7400
16	8884/7337

TRINKET BOX LID

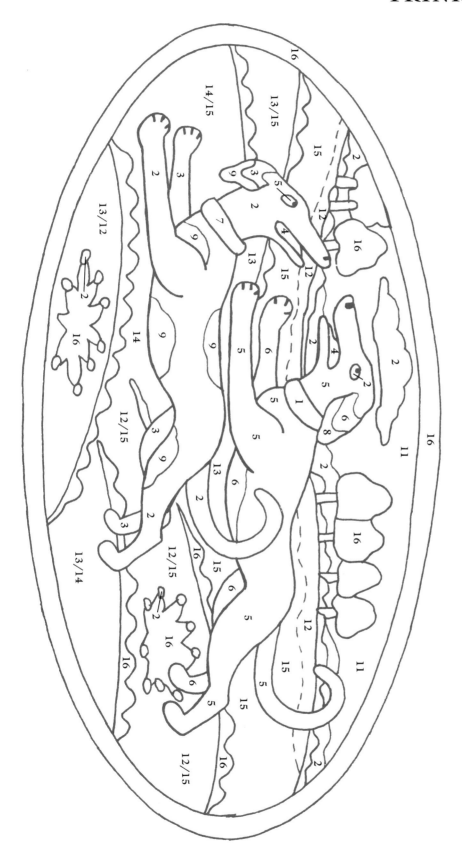

ANCHOR/DMC

1	9648/7533
2	8006/Ecru
3	9614/7120
4	8364/7197
5	8310/7146
6	8262/7356
7	8238/7920
8	9564/7448
9	9388/7421
10	8820/7304
11	8874/7322
12	9212/7351
13	9174/7364
14	8878/7404
15	9058/7400
16	8884/7337

WALKING THE DOG

*T*he fascinating Art Deco period of design and
fashion took its forms from the grace and
harmony of nature. Clothes of the 1920s and 30s
endeavoured to make the wearer appear tall and
elegant. Distortion and exaggeration typified
artistic style. Striking colours and bold effects
contrasted the floral with the geometric. Designers
were widely influenced by the romance of the East,
Egyptian tomb art and the world of The Arabian
Nights. Nothing escaped this dramatic
treatment, not even the image of the cat and dog.
My footstool tapestry "Walking the Dog" is a
tribute to this imaginative era.
For the needlepoint beginner, or for those who wish
to work on their own designs, this style is an ideal
choice with which to start. The lines and shapes
are clean and simple making them easy to draw
and stitch. Fashion books and art posters will
provide you with plenty more ideas.

*SIZE 16¾ × 23in (43 × 59cm). 280 stitches wide × 200
stitches deep.*

MATERIALS

● *12 mesh single or double canvas in white, 23 × 29in
(59 × 74 cm) minimum*

● *Light-coloured waterproof marking pen*

● *Ruler*

● *Size 20 tapestry needle*

● *Tapestry wools as listed on the chart*

● *16¾ × 23in (43 × 59cm) footstool (for supplier see
page 127)*

The design is worked in tent stitch.

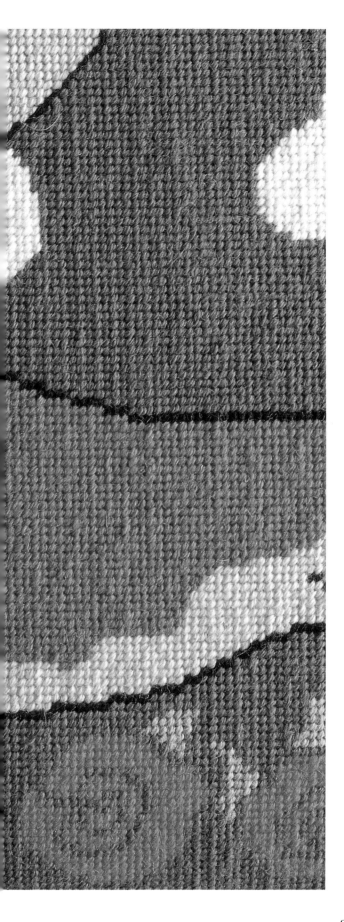

1   The chart on pages 86–7 is split exactly in half. The bold outline of the lady and her dog are filled by flat shapes of colour and small areas of detailed patterns. When using the black wool, take great care to secure all stray ends at the back of the canvas as you work.

2   Lightly draw a line down the centre of the canvas with the pen. Count 140 threads in both directions to give a total width of 280 threads, and 200 threads down. With the ruler draw the outlined rectangle. Prepare the canvas and mount it in a working frame if desired.

3   From the base of the central line, count 43 threads up to the dog's stomach. Then starting in either direction, stitch the outline *only* of the dog until he is complete. Next stitch the black outline *only* of the lady, beginning at the dog's head.

4   Stitch all areas of colour before completing solid areas of black.

5   Neaten back of the work before removing it from the frame. Block if necessary. Turn to pages 124–26 for instructions for making a footstool or a cushion if preferred.

● *Detail of Walking the dog footstool*

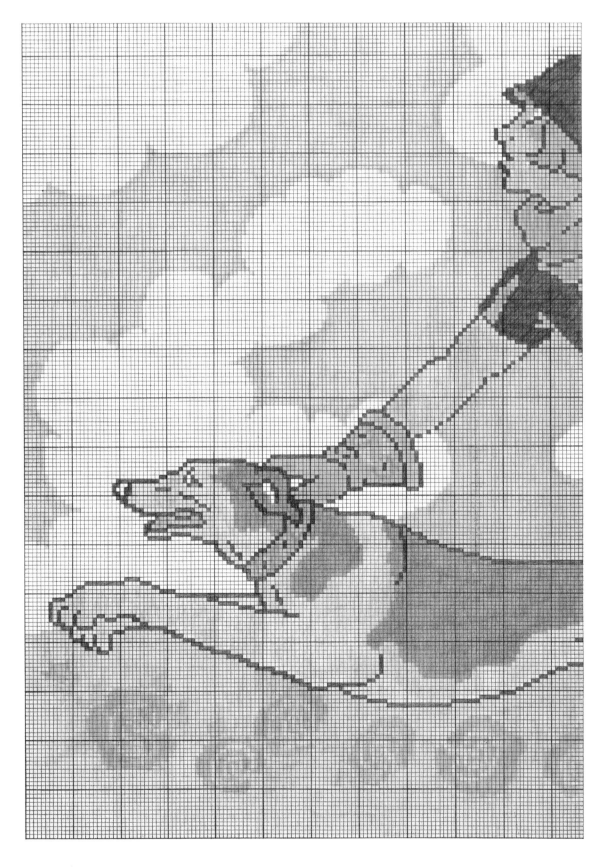

WALKING
THE DOG

8004/Blanc   8016/7727   9274/7680   8900/7690   8604/7244

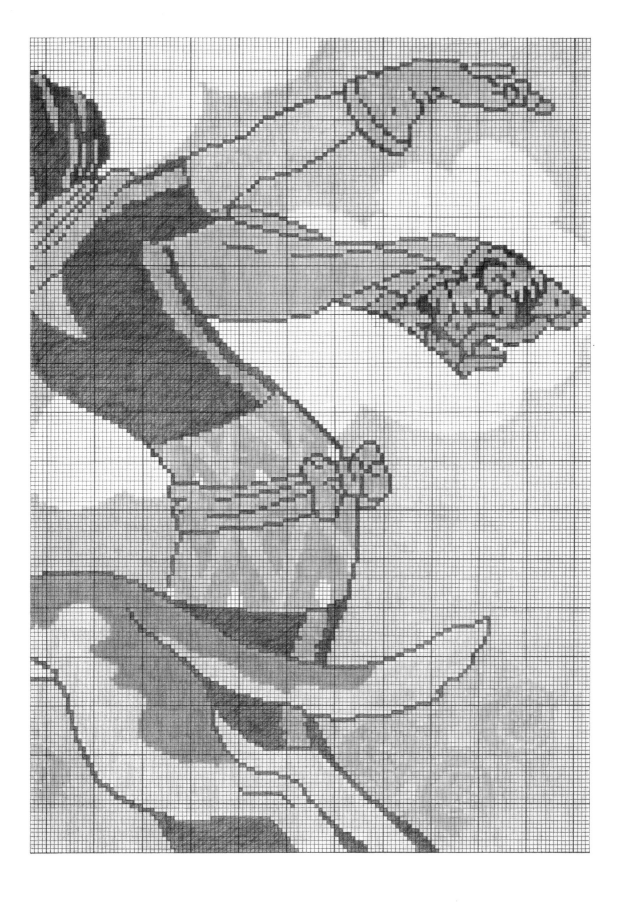

8454/7603   8342/7121   8156/7437   8310/7146   9800/7309

MAURICE AND ·◆· LULU ·◆·

The first of these two designs is a study of my cat Maurice when he was very young and growing fast. The second is of an elusive tabby called Lulu. Ginger tomcats have a reputation for being self-assured, but Maurice is extremely timid and it shows in his eyes. He is here portrayed against the green velvet of his favourite chair. Choosing the right background is very important for any project, and Maurice seems to know exactly which colour makes him look most handsome.

By contrast, Lulu was a flighty, extrovert character who would disappear for days before noisily returning. So my portrait of her is with her mouth open! She never did come back from her last expedition – but you never know. That is the unpredictability of cats.

SIZE *(for each)* 15 × 15in (38 × 38cm). 150 stitches wide × 150 stitches deep.

MATERIALS *(for each)*

● *10 mesh single or double canvas in white or antique, 21 × 21in (53.5 × 53.5cm)*
● *Light-coloured waterproof marking pen*
● *Ruler*
● *Size 18 tapestry needle*
● *Tapestry wools as listed on the charts*
● *19 × 19in (48.5 × 48.5cm) backing fabric (to match background wool colours)*
● *19 × 19in (48.5 × 48.5cm) cotton lining fabric*
● *10in (25.5cm) zip fastener*
● *2⅔yd (2.5m) cord or braid*
● *Polyester filling or 15in (38cm) square cushion pad*

Each design is worked in tent stitch.

1 Study the charts carefully. Whichever you decide to stitch, work in the same way. The background design needs careful stitch counting,

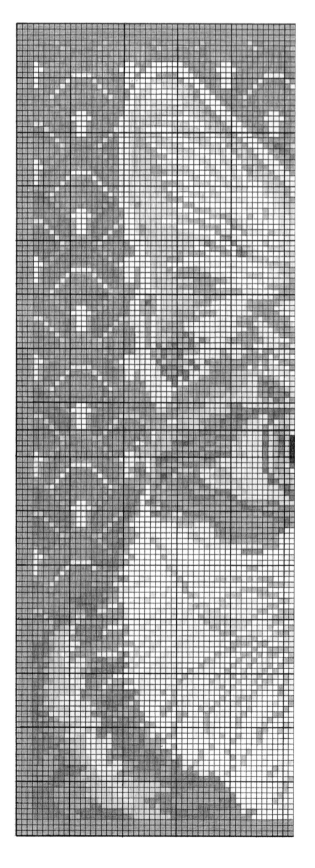

MAURICE

ANCHOR/DMC

8006/Ecru

95402/7171

8038/7503

9552/7917

9554/7173

8306/7124

9556/7922

9564/7459

8342/7121

9162/7549

8878/7335

8604/7244

9774/7282

9800/7309

but don't let any areas worry you unduly. Lightly draw the area to be worked on the canvas using the marking pen and ruler. Count 150 threads across and 150 threads down. Mark the centre point by dividing the width and depth in half. Prepare the canvas and mount it in a working frame if desired. Begin by working either the background or the face.

2 To work the background, start by stitching the simple border in orange/yellow. Count your stitches and double-check before proceeding. Next, tackle the background pattern, keeping the same coloured wool. Follow the diamond trellis, re-counting your stitches if one looks odd. Then use the lighter colour that runs inside. You will soon become familiar with the way these shapes are formed. Finally, fill in the solid background colour in the green/blue. Don't let the cat's whiskers at the bottom confuse you.

3 To work the Cat's Face start from the centre point and count in either direction to work first one eye and then the other. Beginners may find marking the canvas lightly with the pen an aid to counting. Make sure that each eye is the same size and level! Next stitch the surrounding eye markings out to the sides of the face. From the centre point, count down to the nose and stitch it and the mouth. Continue by defining the outline of the chin. Stitch the outline of the ears and complete the markings of the fur. The fur need not be quite so carefully stitch-counted as no two cats have exactly the same markings. Finally, stitch the white and light coloured fur around the cheeks, chin and chest, including the whiskers.

4 Neaten the back of your work before removing it from the frame. Block if necessary and turn to pages 124–26 for instructions on making cushions.

LULU

ANCHOR/DMC

8006/Ecru

9592/7460

9502/7171

8396/7760

8626/7799

9774/7282

8878/7335

9074/7704

8038/7503

9552/7453

9384/7143

9678/7234

9654/7521

9648/7533

Black

93

CREATIVE STITCHES

Traditionally, samplers were worked to show different types of stitches, as well as providing a means for the stitcher to practise technique. This has resulted in a wonderful array of abstract and pictorial works throughout the ages. Join me in a little bit of experimental fun!

One of the main fascinations of canvas-work embroidery is that with one simple stitch you can make quite intricate designs using shades and tones of one colour alone. However, the use of different stitches can also add interest and texture. In the following six pictures, I hope to demonstrate how to create a pictorial sampler using stranded cotton (floss) and various stitches.

The following lists of stranded cotton (floss) colours and stitches are coded using either a number or a letter. These apply to all six charts. Turn to pages 118–22 for the diagrams of each stitch. You will need to refer to these as you work each design.

STITCH KEY

CODE	STITCHES
A	Half cross stitch
B	Straight stitch
C	Long and short stitch
D	Free stitch
E	Satin stitch
F	Gobelin stitch
G	Gobelin filling stitch
	Encroaching gobelin stitch
H	Reversed sloping gobelin stitch
I	Leaf stitch
J	Fan stitch
K	Chequer stitch
L	French knot
M	Florentine stitch
N	Brick stitch
O	Diagonal stitch

COLOUR KEY

CODE NUMBER	COLOUR	ANCHOR	/DMC
1	White	White	Blanc
2	Light grey	849	318
3	Dark grey	235	317
4	Black	403	310
5	Cream	386	3047
6	Buttermilk	300	677
7	Lemon	289	726
8	Bright yellow	291	973
9	Gold	363	436
10	Ochre	307	783
11	Light orange	314	741
12	Dark orange	316	740
13	Rust	339	920
14	Brown	310	433
15	Dark brown	359	801
16	Pale pink	23	225
17	Rose pink	25	776
18	Fuchsia	62	603
19	Deep pink	63	3350
20	Red	46	666
21	Pale blue	128	775
22	Sky blue	144	3325
23	Kingfisher	433	996
24	Royal blue	143	824
25	Mauve	110	333
26	Yellow-green	278	472
27	Sap green	253	3348
28	Grass green	257	703
29	Dark green	212	561
30	Olive green	281	732
31	Deep olive	924	730

DOGS
IN THE PARK

Here is a chance to get to know some dog breeds as well as the stitches. The fun of producing a sampler such as this is that it gives endless scope for variation. You can combine existing stitches or make up your own, as I have done on the Old English Sheep Dog.

SIZE 8¼ × 10in (21 × 25.5cm). 180 stitches wide × 146 stitches deep.

MATERIALS
- *18 mesh single canvas in white, 12 × 14in (31 × 36cm) minimum.*
- *Light-coloured waterproof marking pen*
- *Ruler and masking tape*
- *Size 22 tapestry needle*
- *Stranded cotton (floss) as listed on chart*
- *8¼ × 10in (21 × 25.5cm) cardboard*

1 The chart is drawn in outline only and is exactly to scale. Place the canvas directly on top of the chart and secure in place with pieces of masking tape. Make sure that the canvas is square to the design. Lightly trace the area to be worked on the canvas using the marking pen and ruler. Prepare the canvas and mount it in a working frame if desired.

2 Start by stitching one dog at a time using the colours and stitches suggested. Enjoy working them and forming interesting fur patterns as you stitch.

3 Now stitch the grass and flower border. Next stitch the blue fence and the shrubs and tree behind. Then stitch the sky.

4 Neaten the back of your work before removing it from the frame. Turn to page 125 to see how to lace the piece onto cardboard, then mount and frame it.

DOGS IN THE PARK

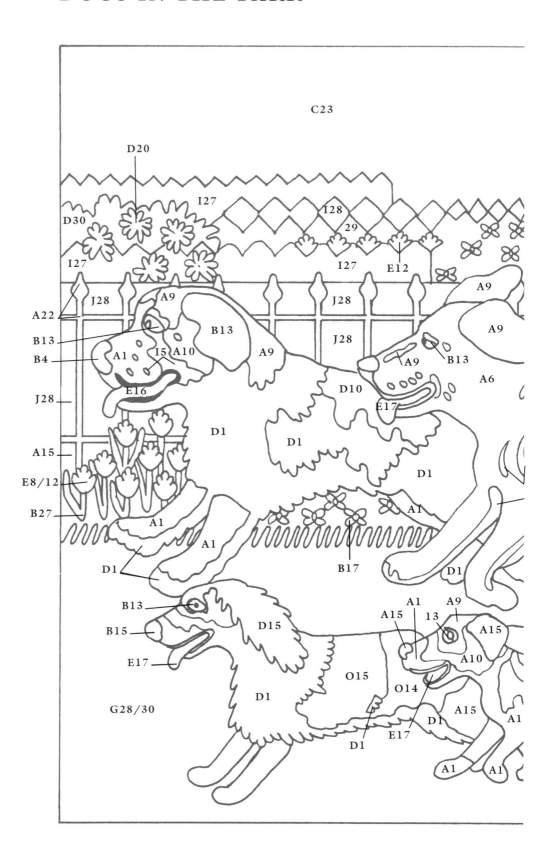

BLACK CAT

Cats have in the past been unfairly associated with bad luck and the occult, and none more than the black cat. The Victorians had a great deal to do with reinstating the black cat's popularity as a domestic pet. This cat is actually bicoloured and is shown sitting pretty among the flowers.

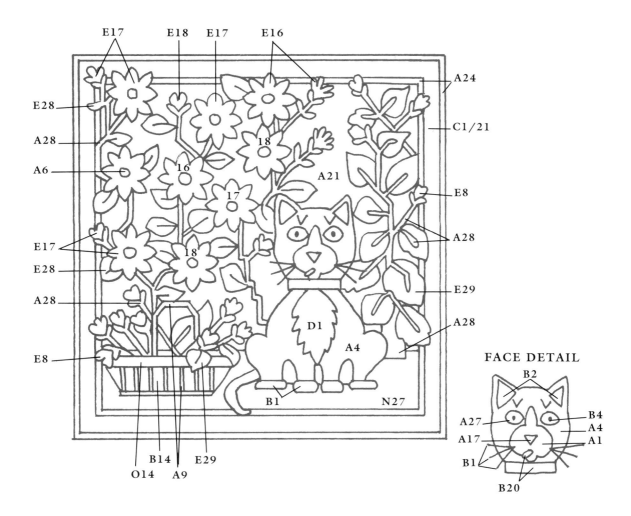

E17　E18　E17　E16

A24

E28

C1/21

A28

A6

A21

E8

17

A28

E17

E28

A28

E29

A28

E8

FACE DETAIL

D1

A4

B1

N27

B14　E29

O14　A9

FACE DETAIL

B2

A27　B4

A4

A17　A1

B1

B20

SIZE 4 × 4in (10 × 10cm). 70 stitches wide × 70 stitches deep.

MATERIALS

- *18 mesh single canvas in white, 8 × 8in (20.5 × 20.5cm) minimum*
- *Light-coloured waterproof marking pen*
- *Ruler and masking tape*
- *Size 22 tapestry needle*
- *Stranded cotton (floss) as listed on chart*
- *4 × 4in (10 × 10cm) cardboard*

1 The chart is drawn in outline only and is exactly to scale. Place the canvas directly on top of the chart and secure in place with pieces of masking tape. Make sure that the canvas is square to the design. Lightly trace the area to be worked on the canvas using the marking pen and ruler. The detail of the cat's face to the side of the chart is to help identify small detailed stitches and colours. Prepare the canvas and mount it in a working frame if desired.

2 Start by stitching the cat and his basket of yellow flowers. Work upwards and stitch the pink flowers and leaves on the left, and the yellow flowers and leaves on the right.

3 Now stitch the blue border and the background sky and grass in the colours suggested. Finally stitch the cat's whiskers.

4 Neaten the back of your work before removing it from the frame. Turn to page 125 for instructions on how to lace the piece onto cardboard, then mount and frame it.

GREY CAT

Cats love to perch in precarious places, often the higher the better. Looking down on the world from such a vantage point is part of their wild past and hunting instinct. It is also a handy refuge from a troublesome dog.

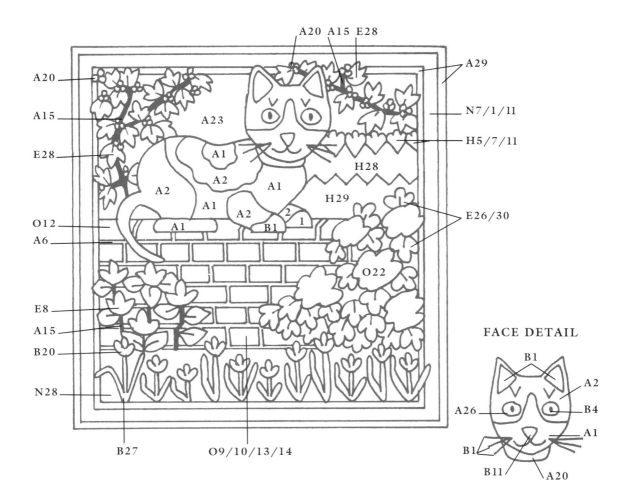

FACE DETAIL

SIZE 4 × 4in (10 × 10cm). 70 stitches wide × 70 stitches deep.

MATERIALS

- *18 mesh single canvas in white, 8 × 8in (20.5 × 20.5cm) minimum*
- *Light-coloured waterproof marking pen*
- *Ruler and masking tape*
- *Size 22 tapestry needle*
- *Stranded cotton (floss) as listed on the chart*
- *4 × 4in (10 × 10cm) cardboard*

1 The chart is drawn in outline only and is exactly to scale. Place the canvas directly on top of the chart and secure in place with pieces of masking tape. Make sure that the canvas is square to the design. Lightly trace the area to be worked on the canvas using the marking pen and ruler. The detail of the cat's face to the side of the chart is to help identify small detailed stitches and colours. Prepare the canvas and mount it in a working frame if desired.

2 Start by stitching the cat and the surrounding flowers. Work each group of plants, enjoying the movement of each type of stitch. Save the bottom row of red flowers for later.

3 Work the wall, background sky and grass, and then the border pattern. Finally, stitch the row of red flowers and the cat's whiskers.

4 Neaten the back of your work before removing it from the frame. Turn to page 125 for instructions on how to lace the piece onto cardboard, then mount and frame it.

GINGER CAT

In the home the cat seems to be fatally attracted to all things forbidden. That precious hand-made rug and that basket of yarn are unlikely to remain neat, tidy and untouched by cat hairs for very long. Cats can be both a nuisance and a pleasure. But while they are contented, the mice will play.

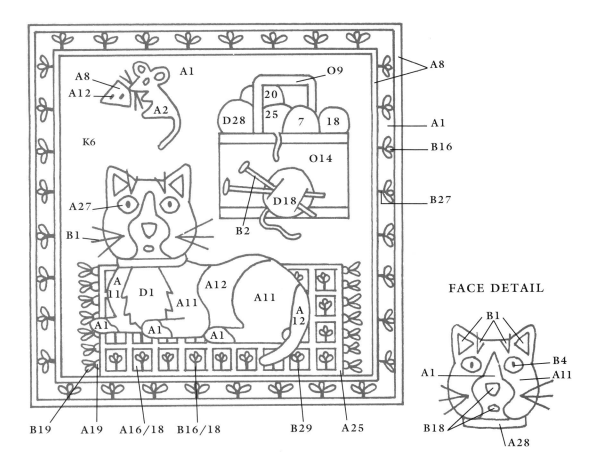

FACE DETAIL

SIZE 4 × 4in (10 × 10cm). 70 stitches wide × 70 stitches deep.

MATERIALS

- 18 mesh single canvas in white, 8 × 8in (20.5 × 20.5cm) minimum
- Light-coloured waterproof marking pen
- Ruler and masking tape
- Size 22 tapestry needle
- Stranded cotton (floss) as listed on the chart
- 4 × 4in (10 × 10cm) cardboard

1 The chart is drawn in outline only and is exactly to scale. Place the canvas directly on top of the chart and secure in place with pieces of masking tape. Make sure that the canvas is square to the design. Lightly trace the area to be worked on the canvas using the marking pen and ruler.

The detail of the cat's face to the side of the chart will prove very useful to help identify small detailed stitches and colours.

Prepare the canvas and mount it in a working frame if desired.

2 Start by stitching the cat and the mat, leaving the cat's whiskers, rug and tassels for later. Stitch the yarns and workbasket and then the large pink ball of yarn and the knitting needles. Enjoy creating the wound-on effect on the wools.

3 Work the background, the mouse and his cheese, and then the border pattern. Finally, stitch the rug, tassels and cat's whiskers.

4 Neaten the back of your work before removing it from the frame. Turn to page 125 for instructions on how to lace the piece onto cardboard, then mount and frame it.

SIAMESE CATS

One of the legends about this oriental cat is that the kink in its tail was formed
when the princess of Siam hung her rings on her favourite cat's tail and tied a knot to keep them safe.
Other features that set them apart from other cats are their non-retractable
claws (like dogs), their piercing blue eyes and their distinctive miaow.

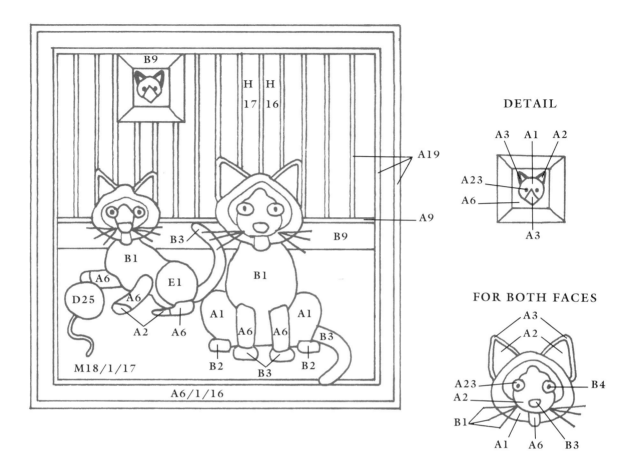

DETAIL

FOR BOTH FACES

SIZE 4×4in (10×10cm). 70 stitches wide × 70 stitches deep.

MATERIALS

18 mesh single canvas in white, 8×8in (20.5×20.5cm) minimum

- *Light-coloured waterproof marking pen*
- *Ruler and masking tape*
- *Size 22 tapestry needle*
- *Stranded cotton (floss) as listed on chart*
- *4×4in (10×10cm) cardboard*

1 The chart is drawn in outline only and is exactly to scale. Place the canvas directly on top of the chart and secure in place with pieces of masking tape. Make sure that the canvas is square to the design. Lightly trace the area to be worked on the canvas using the marking pen and ruler.

The details of the cat's face and the framed portrait to the side of the chart are to help identify small detailed stitches and colours.

Prepare the canvas and mount it in a working frame if desired.

2 Start by stitching both of the cats and then the ball of yarn, leaving the whiskers until last for obvious reasons.

3 Stitch the background, walls, floor and the little framed portrait. Enjoy working the smooth, satin effects and watching the picture take shape. Next stitch the simple border pattern and finally work the cats' whiskers.

4 Neaten the back of your work before removing it from the frame. Turn to page 125 for instructions on how to lace the piece onto cardboard, them mount and frame it.

CAT WITH FLOWERS

It is curious how most alley cats seem to be black and white. Many much-loved pets are recognisable by individual markings, such as this cat's beauty spot. Cats love to be in long grass. Town cats, however, will often take cover among flower pots and window boxes.

SIZE 9⅝ × 10⅝in (24.5 × 27cm). 193 stitches wide × 173 stitches deep.

MATERIALS

- *18 mesh single canvas in white, 14 × 15in (35.5 × 38cm) minimum*
- *Light-coloured waterproof marking pen*
- *Ruler and masking tape*
- *Size 22 tapestry needle*
- *Stranded cotton (floss) as listed on chart*
- *9⅝ × 10⅝in (24.5 × 27cm) cardboard*

1 The chart is drawn in outline only and is exactly to scale. Place the canvas directly on top of the chart and secure in place with pieces of masking tape. Make sure that the canvas is square to the design. Lightly trace the area to be worked on the canvas using the marking pen and ruler. Match up the base of the border.
  Prepare the canvas and mount it in a working frame if desired.

2 Start by stitching the large flowers using the colours and stitches suggested, completing one head at a time before progressing on to the leaves, stems and smaller flowers.

3 Stitch the cat, grass and sky and the diamond-patterned border. Finally, stitch the cat's whiskers.

4 Neaten the back of your work before removing it from the frame. Turn to page 125 for instructions on how to lace the piece onto cardboard, then mount and frame it.

CAT
WITH FLOWERS

MATERIALS, EQUIPMENT AND TECHNIQUES

There is no mystery to starting needlepoint tapestry. All you need is a length of canvas and suitable yarns and needles. Experience will be your best guide to selecting materials and developing a good technique. Professional designers can give invaluable advice and personal expertise, but there are no hard and fast rules. Studying both old and new examples of needlework is a fascinating way to learn. Observing the different effects achieved by mixing and matching materials is part of its charm.

MATERIALS

Among the many canvases and yarns available, there is an element of choice that will determine how your work will look on completion. The ultimate purpose of the finished work is the first consideration for any designer. Some decisions are made based on suitability of use, others on personal colour preference or individual working techniques. Most designer projects will state which yarns, canvas and needles to use, but it is worth getting to know the alternatives.

YARNS

A variety of yarns have been especially designed by manufacturers for working on canvas, with different textures, thicknesses and durability and in

● *Materials: canvas, frames, yarns and needles. Your choice will be reflected in the individual look of your completed work*

a myriad of colours. Each has its own distinctive features and uses, creating many stunning effects. Apart from their appearance, yarns must be chosen to cover the canvas comfortably, without gaps showing between stitches.

There are four distinctive types of yarn: tapestry wool, crewel wool, Persian yarn and soft embroidery thread. The yarn most commonly used for cushion, rug and footstool designs is tapestry wool, a softly twisted 4-ply yarn similar in weight to knitting yarn but more hard-wearing. The vast choice of shades, tints and tones are dye-fast and mothproof. Most are supplied in lengths of 8–10 metres (8¾–11 yards) called skeins. Selected colours (including black and white) are referred to as grounding and supplied in larger quantities called a hank. A single strand of tapestry wool will comfortably cover any canvas up to 10 mesh. Larger-mesh canvas needs to be stitched with double lengths of yarn.

Crewel wool is a fine yet firmly twisted 2-ply wool. To cover a 10-mesh canvas requires three strands and a careful technique to ensure the threads lie evenly when worked. One or two strands of crewel wool will bulk up tapestry wool for larger-mesh canvas, creating some interesting effects. It is well worth experimenting.

More lustrous is Persian yarn, which is supplied as three loosely twisted 2-ply strands that can easily be separated to mix with other yarns. Colours are limited but its lovely texture is ideal for rug fringing.

Among the variety of finer threads is stranded cotton or embroidery floss. Made up of six gently twisted strands, it has a luscious sheen like silk and comes in an ever-increasing range of colours. It is ideal for creating striking pictorial designs on smaller-mesh canvas. Used double it adds an interesting contrast against wools worked on canvas up to 10 mesh, and a single strand makes ideal cat whiskers. Other fine threads include perlé or mercerised cotton, cotton à broder and soft matte embroidery cotton, as well as fine metallic threads for special effects.

CANVAS

Canvas is made from machine-woven cotton or polished linen. Individual threads form an even grid of open squares referred to as the gauge, mesh or thread count. Canvas varies by the numbers of threads it contains per inch (2.5cm). This will determine the stitch size and overall dimensions of the completed work. For example, a design worked in tent stitch on a 10-mesh canvas will require fewer stitches per inch (2.5cm) and be larger in scale than if it is worked on a 14-mesh canvas. The first choice may be easier to work; however, with the second there is the opportunity to incorporate finer detail within the same design.

There is a wide range of mesh sizes available from 3, 5 or 7 mesh canvas for bold rug designs; 10, 11, 12, 13 or 14 mesh most commonly chosen for cushion and footstool designs, and 16 to 32 mesh canvas for fine work called *petit point*.

There are three main types of canvas on which to work: single (mono), double (Penelope), and interlock. The choice is largely a matter of personal preference. The most conventional is mono, or single thread, canvas. This is composed of individual strong threads woven vertically and horizontally, one over the other, to form a sturdy canvas. Its main advantage is that it is strong and hard-wearing, an ideal choice for upholstery. It also comes in the complete range of mesh sizes. Its smooth polished appearance is attractive for beginners as the squares are clearly defined and easy on the eye. Its starched quality gives finished designs a neat, flat look, but this stiffness can sometimes be a disadvantage. Those who prefer stitching from the front using one hand in an embroiderer's style will find this canvas difficult to work on. It can also be tough and unyielding to hand-sew when it is being made into shaped cushions.

The most authentic type of canvas, similar to that used by the Victorians, is Penelope, or double thread, canvas. Woven in the same way as single thread canvas but composed of two finer threads running parallel, it is softer and more pliable to work on. Its great advantage is that the double threads can be eased apart to allow a variety of stitches and yarns to be used. It is ideal for experimental and creative pieces, and my personal favourite. It is easier to stretch over footstools and can impart a pleasing antique softness to finished work. One disadvantage is that threads can be torn and the surface creased if it is handled roughly. Respect this canvas by working on a frame if possible and employ a good stitching technique.

The latest form of canvas to evolve is double interlock canvas. Similar in looks to double-threaded canvas, its threads pass through one another and are locked in position, giving it some of the advantages of double-thread canvas combined with the firmer quality of single-thread canvas. It is ideal for beginners. Its disadvantages are its limited mesh size and its availability in white only.

Canvas is generally available in a range of tints from white, cream, yellow to a light brown often called "antique". Choose the colour of canvas depending on the dominant colour of yarns used; light colours require a white canvas. Dark colours are best worked on antique canvas. White canvas will usually show through a large area of black yarn; however, white yarn worked on tinted canvas is perfectly acceptable.

Canvas is supplied by the yard in a range of widths. Allow at least 3in (7.5cm) margin all the way around the design, choosing the nearest width to save unnecessary wastage. Always cut neatly along a line of threads.

Woven fabrics such as Aida are designed especially for embroidery and counted cross stitch where the background is left largely unworked.

To prepare canvas prior to stitching, bind raw edges with masking tape to prevent fraying and snagging of yarns. Alternatively fold down approximately $\frac{1}{3}$in (1cm) in from each edge and sew loosely in place. The canvas is now ready to be mounted in a frame for stitching.

EQUIPMENT

To keep your work from stretching out of shape, it is advisable to attach the canvas to a frame. This will enable you to work with both hands and also help retain the canvas's fresh starchiness. Available in a variety of widths, there are basically two types of working frames, the roller-ended or travel frame and the straight-sided slate or scroll frame. A length of cloth tape is firmly stapled to the top and bottom bars, onto which the ends of the canvas should be neatly stitched. To achieve a taut surface on which to work, simply roll surplus canvas around the top and/or bottom bars, unwinding or tightening as required. If the canvas sags while you are working, lace the sides of the canvas to the sides of the frame.

Tapestry needles differ from conventional sewing needles, with a blunt rounded end and an elongated eye. Sizes range from 24 to 13 (the smaller the number, the larger the needle). You should never have to force or tug at a needle when stitching, as this will damage both canvas and yarn. Generally, the higher the needle size, the smaller the canvas mesh. Above all, the needle should be comfortable to use.

A permanent waterproof marking pen is an invaluable piece of equipment when you are faced with a blank piece of canvas. It can help with thread counting, plotting dimensions and transferring designs. Make sure that the colour used is light enough to see, but not so dark that it shows through your stitching. Never use a water-soluble pen.

In addition, ruler, tape measure, dressmaker pins, sewing thread, masking tape and embroidery and fabric scissors are useful items. Occasionally needed are stretching frame and blotting paper, water sprayer, small upholstery tacks and spray starch. These items are especially useful when your needlework has become badly distorted.

TECHNIQUES

Developing a good stitching technique will come with practice. To avoid bad habits such as untidy backs and uneven stitches requires just a little care and patience. Always neaten the back of your work as you go. Lumps and bumps will spoil the surface of your stitching and stray ends will invariably work their way through to the front. Yarn and thread will occasionally twist when stitching. If it does, simply let the yarn hang from the back of your work and untwist by itself, with the needle acting as a weight. Stitches should be neither too tight nor too loose, covering the canvas comfortably without distortion. Whether you prefer to work on your lap, stitching from the front with one hand, or on a frame using both hands to work the needle back and forth, is entirely your choice. Just remember to relax and enjoy.

STRETCHING

Needlework that has become badly distorted, especially if it is hand-held, will need stretching back into shape, sometimes referred to as blocking or setting. You will need a simple wooden frame or a piece of board at least as big as your canvas, as well as a clean sheet of blotting paper, drawing pins or thumb tacks, a ruler and/or template, and a water sprayer.

1. Position blotting paper over the frame or on the board.
2. Place the needlework on top, face down.
3. Lightly spray the back of the work with water.
4. Gently stretch into shape, pinning at regular intervals around the canvas border.
5. Check that the work is square with the aid of a paper template cut to desired shape, re-spraying and re-pinning the piece if necessary.
6. Allow to dry naturally.
7. Before removing, lightly spray the back with a recommended fabric starch.

DESIGNING FOR YOURSELF

While many stitchers are happy working from one kit to the next, the time may come when prepared canvases start to lose their appeal. Discontented with restricted colour schemes and impersonal designs, you may have found yourself making minor alterations. Now is the time to take the plunge and design for yourself. You really don't have to be an artist or a technical expert. What you will need is loads of enthusiasm. Your confidence will grow with experience and encouraging comments. An eye for detail, colour and form will come with time. So will the desire to improve your stitching skills.

Creating your own needlepoint tapestry is extremely satisfying. There is an element of risk and surprise that is very exciting. Never knowing exactly how each project will evolve is like turning the pages of a thrilling book. Once you're hooked, you will not want to put it down until you have finished. So be warned!

Be prepared to experiment and don't expect to get it right first time. Designing for yourself will give you freedom of choice and a chance for self-expression. Ask yourself what you want to achieve, but don't be too ambitious. Start with something relatively simple to boost your confidence and progress from there.

First, select your subject. Inspiration is all around us: a collection of favourite greetings cards and photographs, snippets from magazines, even pieces of china or family ornaments can provide source material. Often the more unusual and far-removed from needlepoint the source material is, the more original your work will be.

Try not to copy exactly, but be selective. Discriminate between parts of a design you like and those you don't. A good design should have interesting detail without being too fussy, be well balanced within the space provided, and never be overpowered by a large background.

Once you have found your project, decide how you want it to look: size, stitch and its ultimate use. Make it fairly small to begin with. If it is too large or complicated, you are liable to abandon it at the first sign of its "going wrong". Your initial stitches may look like nothing on earth, but persevere; it will be worth it in the end. At this stage, a sample of different size canvas will be useful so that you can practise to see which threads or stitches look best.

Next, you will need to draw your design. A bold outline is all that is required; your stitches and coloured yarns will be producing the detail. Whether it is traced or freehand, draw it to the size needed on graph paper or directly onto your canvas. To enlarge a design, place a sheet of tracing paper on top and secure it in position with masking tape. Draw the perimeter of the areas you want, find the centre and divide it into equal quarters. Divide each quarter again to form a grid. This will break the design into manageable sections from which to copy. Now trace the outline of your chosen design. On a sheet of paper (preferably graph paper with the same number of squares per inch (2.5cm) as your canvas) copy the grid to the size wanted and fill in the outline of the design boldly, making any alterations you think necessary. To transfer it onto your canvas, place it on top of your scaled drawing and trace using a light-coloured waterproof pen. Use a different colour pen for any adjustments.

● *Subtly changing shades, tints and tones allow you to play with various colour themes*

The choice of yarn or thread colours is crucial to a successful design. Life-like effects can be achieved if you use a wide range of subtly changing shades, tints and tones. You can never really have too many colours, provided that they harmonise. Colour is a very personal thing; we all view it in different ways. The colours you select will be individual to you. If you are confident using paints or crayons, you may like to play with various colour themes. Look back at your source materials to get ideas. Alternatively, go straight to the yarns themselves. Yarn manufacturers produce comprehensive shade cards that remove the guess-work from selecting. I suggest that you

make a list at home and purchase only one skein of each colour at this stage.

Once you start stitching, you may find some colours look different. There are many reasons for this. As light alters, so will the appearance of your yarns, particularly in artificial light, so keep them in a recognisable order when working. Also, colours viewed individually will look different when placed against others. Strong shades can dominate subtle tints, draining their delicate hues. So be prepared to make an occasional colour substitution. This is something many artists are aware of when painting. Colour values can be learnt but the element of surprise can often lead to happy accidents and some unplanned effects. Finally, the stitches themselves will form gentle shadows, making colours appear fractionally darker than they first seemed.

STITCHES

The type of stitch you use will depend entirely on how you approach your design. Using one simple stitch only, such as tent stitch, will enable you to devote your attention to colour, shape and detail, while a variety of stitches such as those used for conventional pictorial samples will add texture and interest. An encyclopedia of needlepoint and embroidery stitches is a must. It can be all too easy to develop careless stitching habits when concentrating on your design. At first your mind will be in a whirl trying to juggle good technique with artistic creativity. However, I hope that you will soon find working your very own needlepoint designs a thoroughly rewarding experience.

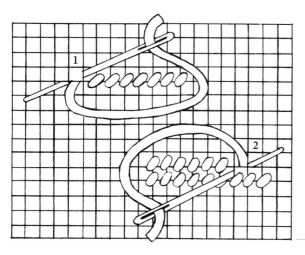

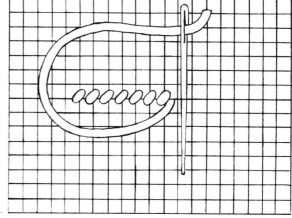

TENT STITCH

Small diagonal stitches worked over one section of canvas threads in the same direction, forming long diagonal stitches at back of work. Also known as gros, petit point or continental stitch. Ideal for cushions and footstools.

1. Work horizontally from right to left. Bring needle out and upwards diagonally to the right along one canvas thread. Insert needle. Bring downwards diagonally from behind, two canvas threads along to the left. Repeat as before.

2. On the next row, work left to right. Work diagonally downwards and along one canvas thread to the left. Insert needle. Bring upwards diagonally from behind, two canvas threads to the right. Bring needle out and repeat to the end of row.

HALF-CROSS STITCH

Similar in appearance to tent stitch but uses less yarn, forming one vertical stitch at back of work. Less hardwearing, it is ideal for small pictorial designs.

1. Working from left to right, bring needle out and upwards diagonally to the right along one canvas thread. Insert needle, bring out vertically downwards. Continue as before.

2. Second row, turn canvas upside down and work as before.

118

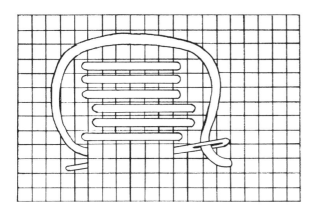

STRAIGHT STITCH

Worked horizontally or vertically to form a block
of straight stitches. Covers canvas quickly for
landscapes and portrait pictures.
1. Bring needle out and along to required length.
Insert needle, bring out again next to first stitch
and continue, altering the length of each stitch as
necessary to form a block of straight stitch.

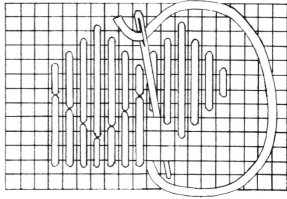

LONG-AND-SHORT STITCH

Ideal for making geometric shaped patterns for
pictorial borders, etc.
1. Work horizontally, bringing needle out and
vertically upwards to required length. Insert
needle, bring out vertically downwards next to
first stitch. Gradually decrease or increase the
length of each stitch to form diamonds or
triangles.
2. Continue second row in reverse to fit evenly
into previous row. Always take needle down into a
row of previously worked stitches.

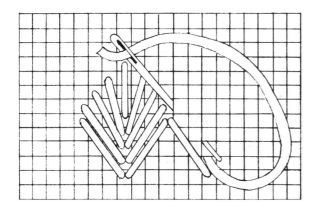

LEAF STITCH

Two lines of diagonal stitches set at right angles
and shaped into uniform leaf patterns. Ideal for
floral pictures.
1. Insert needle from left to right diagonally,
three canvas threads across and four threads
down. Work two or more stitches before gradually
tapering to a point. Reverse direction to form
other half of leaf.
2. Repeat pattern, interlocking the leaf formation
with each row.

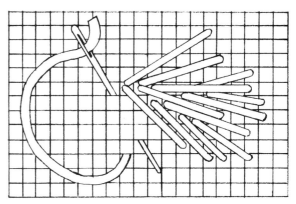

FREE STITCH

Straight stitches which change direction
haphazardly for rough textures such as dog's fur.
1. Bring needle out and along to required length
and direction. Insert needle, bring out again next
to original point. Second stitch can change length
and direction, or even overlap first stitch.
2. Make sure canvas is thoroughly covered.

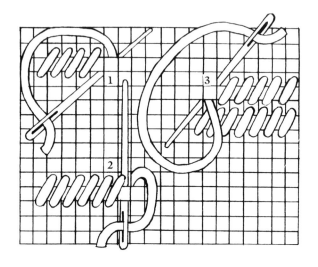

GOBELIN STITCH

Similar to tent stitch, but passing over two rows of threads to create an elongated, sloping appearance.

1. Work from left to right, bringing needle out diagonally down over two horizontal rows of canvas threads. Insert needle one thread along. Repeat.

2. Next row, bring needle up vertically to top of previous row.

3. Working from right to left, stitch as before.

GOBELIN FILLING STITCH

Upright long stitches that interlock. Worked horizontally in even rows. Ideal for an all-over background pattern.

1. Bring needle out and vertically up over six rows of canvas threads. Insert needle and bring out level with top of first stitch, two threads along. Continue.

2. Second row, work in opposite direction, fitting stitches evenly into first row as shown.

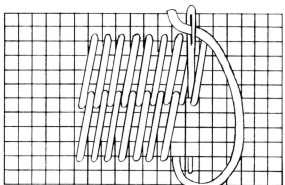

ENCROACHING GOBELIN STITCH

Similar to gobelin filling stitch but worked at a slight angle and closer together. Ideal for grass effects.

1. From right to left, bring needle out and diagonally across one and down five canvas threads. Insert needle and bring out vertically upwards.

2. Work second row from left to right, vertically down and diagonally upwards. Overlap each stitch with the previous row by one horizontal thread.

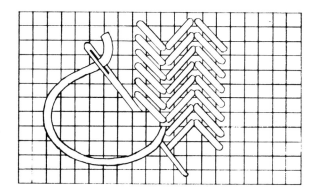

REVERSED SLOPING GOBELIN STITCH

Two vertical lines of diagonal stitches set at right angles to each other. A good all-over pattern.

1. Work first row vertically sloping stitch down to the right, over two canvas threads across and down.

2. Work second row in reverse.

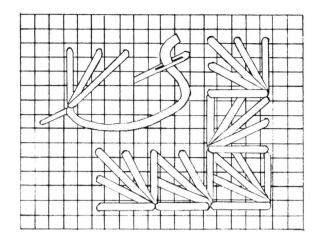

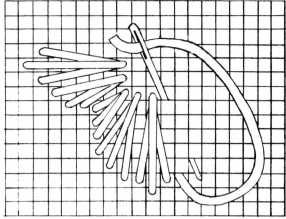

FAN STITCH

Straight stitches radiating from one point over a square block of canvas threads. Creates good leaf patterns.

1. Work horizontally or vertically from bottom left of a block of four canvas threads. Radiate five straight stitches like a "fan".

2. Stitch second row in reverse, radiating from bottom right. Continue alternating, changing colours if required.

SATIN STITCH

An overlapping straight stitch similar in concept to a truncated fan stitch, it gently graduates to create smooth shapes such as flower petals.

1. Work horizontally, vertically or diagonally, bringing needle out, along and back in. Bring needle out from the original hole again and move along one canvas thread to go back in. Repeat as necessary, then move around the shape being stitched as needed. Ensure stitches lie flat and fairly taut, neatly touching without gaps.

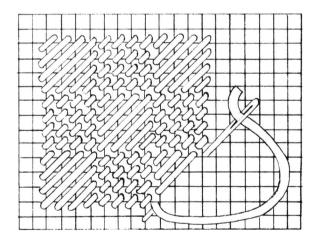

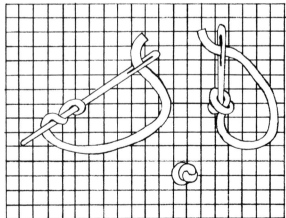

CHEQUER STITCH

A mixture of tent and diagonal straight stitches worked in even blocks of squares. Effective all-over pattern, colours and textures can be varied.

1. Work horizontally from left to right, alternating squares of tent stitch and diagonal stitches. Cover four vertical and four horizontal canvas threads in each block.

FRENCH KNOT

An embroidery-based stitch used to create three-dimensional interest for pictorial and floral work.

1. Bring needle out and twist yarn several times around needle depending on size required, usually one or two times. Insert needle back where it emerged from to form the French knot.

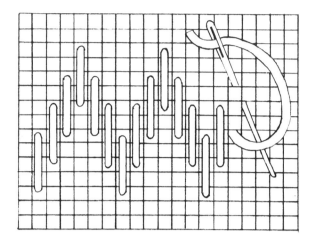

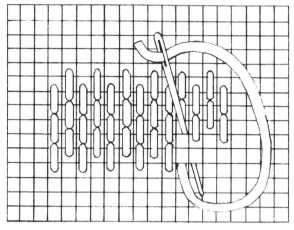

FLORENTINE STITCH

Also known as Bargello. Uniform straight stitches graduating into a zig-zag pattern. Changing colours can create stunning geometric effects.
1. Work over two or more horizontal threads in a regular stepping sequence of your choice. Each row can use stitches of a different length.

BRICK STITCH

Small upright stitches forming a neat, regular pattern. This is a very useful stitch.
1. Work vertically over two horizontal canvas threads, one up and one down in a stepped sequence across each row.

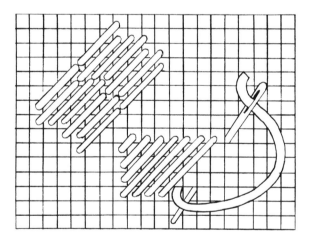

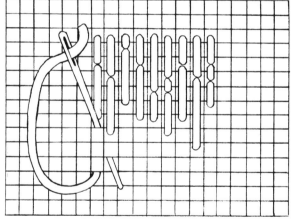

DIAGONAL STITCH

Straight stitches slope in the same direction to create many effects.
1. Start from top left and work to bottom right of area to be covered. Make a series of diagonal stitches over two, three and four canvas threads.
2. Second row should fit neatly into first row.

RANDOM LONG STITCH

The haphazard use of long and short stitches form this versatile stitch. Stitch lengths are dictated by colour and pictorial design. Ideal for fine detail and for covering background areas quickly.
1. Work rows using vertical stitches. Vary stitch lengths over one, two or more horizontal canvas threads as required.
2. The following rows should fit neatly into first while each stitch length is still being varied. Avoid forming regular patterns such as zig-zags, which can be distracting.

FINISHING THE PROJECTS

Having lavished many hours on completing your needlepoint tapestry, it is absolutely fatal to then put it away unmade. A drawer or cupboard that accumulates such pieces of needlework is a sorry place indeed. Yet it's amazing how many needleworkers feel that once the design is done, the fun ends. This is most definitely not the case. Indeed you should be proud of your achievement, however modest. Turning it into something useful, such as a cushion, glasses case, footstool or framed picture, can only enhance it. The pleasure will continue as you try to match your work to an interesting frame, or find a backing material that looks just right. Another stumbling block appears to be the word "sewing". The trick is to approach the subject from the easiest angle – and never look for difficulties. Therefore, a zip fastener is merely two lengths of tape, a circular cushion means there are no edges and a square cushion has only four sides to join! So, having hopefully inspired you with confidence, I urge you to thread that needle and enjoy "making-up".

SELECTING MATERIAL

When choosing a backing fabric, always take your finished needlework, or the wools used, with you. Select a fabric which is similar in weight, such as a furnishing fabric. Don't be tempted to use dressmaking fabrics as they are too lightweight and less hard-wearing.

Cotton velvet is an ideal choice for backing Victorian-style designs. It looks authentic and is available in a good choice of rich colours. Also, look for cost-saving remnants of otherwise expensive designs. The plusher the fabric, the better the finished results. For the "Maurice" cushion (pages 88–93), I used a reproduction of a nineteenth-century William Morris design printed on heavy cotton. Its orange and green shades matched the tapestry wools perfectly. Don't feel that you have to restrict yourself to plain fabrics either. A pattern which reflects the shades and tones in your work will look stunning.

Equally, the use of decorative cord or braid should enhance, not distract from, the overall effect – like a picture frame. There are a wide range to choose from, some plain and some with twists of multi-coloured bands. It's all a matter of personal taste, so remember to take your work with you and see how one looks when compared to another. Provided that the colours are in harmony, you may find yourself spoilt for choice. The tasselled braid used on the "Buccaneer Cat" circular cushion (pages 66–9) was a lucky find in a remnant box.

I would always recommend that you line the back of your work with a plain cotton lining material. First, it will protect the wools from the filling used to shape it; second, it will keep surplus unworked canvas neatly tucked away and make it easier to handle when attaching cord and zip fastening. Third, it will make your cushion more hard-wearing for the years to come, and finally, it will hide a multitude of sins!

Attaching a zip fastener to the base of a cushion will look far more professional than any other form of fastening (no matter how easy it looks to

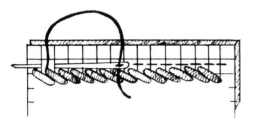

Backstitch seams on back of canvas

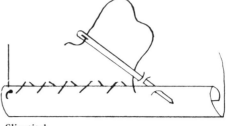

Slipstitch

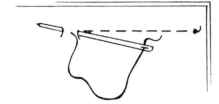

Backstitch

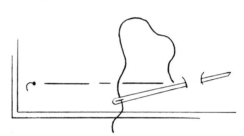

Hem stitch

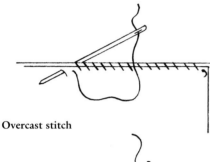

Overcast stitch

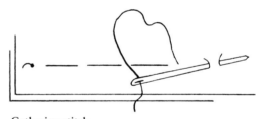

Tacking (Basting) stitch

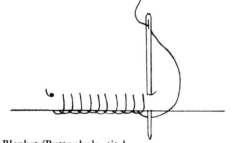

Blanket/Buttonhole stitch

Gathering stitch

apply). Match the colour to your backing material, darker rather than lighter in shade so that it "disappears" when inserted.

Finally, don't forget to purchase matching sewing thread for the backing material, zip fastener and cord or braid.

SEWING TECHNIQUES

Hand-sewing in backstitch is, I find, preferable to machine sewing. You can use the thread double for additional strength, and you can make a much closer line of stitching. This is achieved by working from the canvas side, sewing along the row of canvas holes at the edge of your needlepoint tapestry. Sewing in this way is incredibly easy and produces a very neat seam.

Neaten all raw edges with either blanket stitch, buttonhole or zig-zag stitch by hand or with a sewing machine. A zip fastener is also best hand-sewn in position to keep stitching invisible from the right side. All cords and braid should similarly be hand-sewn, stitching all the way around the outside of the design using a curved needle if desired. They should not be pulled tight when attaching, but make sure that cord does not unwind as you work. Also, note that all newly cut ends must be securely bound with thread or tape to prevent fraying.

MAKING A CUSHION

1. Place needlework on top of backing material, right sides together. Pin and trim, leaving a 2in

(5cm) border on three sides, plus 3in (7.5cm) for a hem on the fourth side.

2. Using the waterproof pen mark the position of the zip fastener on the canvas centrally at the base of the design. Also mark 1½in (4cm) at the base left of the design for insertion of cord.

3. Tack (baste) all around and remove pins.

4. With matching thread, stitch on the canvas side as described earlier. Do not stitch the marked areas. Remove tacking.

5. Pin lining to the back of canvas. At the base, turn under the surplus canvas and lining material to form a neat edge. Pin together and sew using small overcasting stitches. Fold over the base of the backing material to form a hem; pin in position. Sew using slipstitch, picking up as few threads as possible from the backing material as you work.

6. Trim the remaining three sides to within ½in (1cm) of sewing. Cut corners diagonally to prevent bulk. Neaten all raw edges using blanket or zig-zag stitches. Remove all pins.

7. Place one length of the opened zip fastener along the base and pin. Tack, then backstitch it into position. Make sure that the tongue faces inwards. Do the same for the other side. Remove pins and tacking.

8. Turn your cushion right side out. Carefully ease out corners using a blunt implement. Check that the zip works.

9. Attach cord or braid by first inserting one end approximately 1½in (4cm) into the gap at the base. Secure it in place with a few stitches before sewing all the way around. Form loops or attach tassels at each corner and securely stitch in place. Finish by pulling surplus cord or braid through the same gap as when you started. Stitch firmly in position and check that the ends are securely bound inside the cushion.

10. Complete by inserting a cushion pad or stuff it with washable filling to the desired shape. Last, place a strip of lining material along the opening. This keeps the stuffing from getting caught in the teeth of the zip when you close it.

Circular and shaped cushions

Follow the basic instructions for making a cushion, but before neatening the raw edges, cut V-shapes at regular intervals to within ⅛in (3mm) of the stitching. For shaped cushions such as the Gallé cats and Staffordshire dogs, you need to do this only on inward-facing curves.

Neaten all raw edges carefully to prevent fraying. Continue basic cushion-making instructions until you are ready to turn the piece right side out. Extra attention should be paid to turning ear and head shapes. Similarly, when stuffing, make sure these areas are well filled and rounded. Backing material should be smooth without any wrinkles.

LACING PICTURES ONTO BOARD

It is desirable to lace your needlework onto a piece of board before having it mounted and framed. This will keep your work flat and lightly stretched. Stiff cardboard also works well.

1. Cut the board to the same size as the needlework, making sure it is perfectly square.

2. Lay your needlework face down on a table and place the board on top.

3. Fold the surplus canvas over, making sure the corners are neat and flat. If desired, insert pins along the edge to hold the work in place.

4. Using strong thread, lace the top and bottom of the canvas together, pulling tight as you go. Repeat for the sides. When the lacing is sufficiently taut, stitch down the corners neatly.

5. Your work is now ready to be mounted and framed.

PENNY FARTHING CLOCK
(pp 74–7)

Your work must be laced onto a piece of board before fitting the clock mechanism and ultimately being framed. The mechanism can be purchased quite cheaply from most craft shops. It consists of a square plastic box that houses a single battery and concealed clock workings. The central stem has a removable screw onto which a choice of hands can be fitted.

1. Lay your needlework face down on a table, placing the cardboard specified for this project on top.

2. Fold the surplus canvas over and pin it in position. Turn the needlework over and mark the position of the centre of the wheel with the marking pen.

3. Remove the needlework and pierce a hole through the cardboard where marked. The hole should be large enough to accommodate the central stem of the clock mechanism with the screw removed.

4. Reposition the needlework on the cardboard, making sure that the corners are neat and flat.

Lace the top and bottom of the canvas with strong thread, pulling tight as you go. Repeat for the sides. Stitch down the corners.

5. Fit the clock mechanism to the back, gently pushing the central stem through the hole.

6. From the front, attach first the hour hand and then the minute hand. Screw in place.

7. Check that the hands are not obstructed by any stray threads before setting the time and inserting the battery.

8. Frame as desired.

CIRCULAR FOOTSTOOL AND PINCUSHION
(pp 62–5 and pp 70–2)

The footstool used for the project on pages 62–5 and the pincushion project on pages 70–72 differ only in scale. Attach both in the same way.

1. Trim surplus canvas to within 3in (7.5cm) of the needlework for the footstool and 1½ (4cm) for the pincushion.

2. Using a strong thread, take a gathering stitch all the way around the edge of the canvas. Stitch two separate rows for the footstool.

3. Unscrew calico (muslin) pad from its base.

4. Lay your needlework face down on a table, positioning the calico pad on top.

5. Pull the drawstrings to gather the canvas evenly. This will require a little patience for the footstool. It may be helpful to insert drawing pins or upholstery tacks as you gather. Leave overnight to stretch before doing anything else.

6. Continue gathering, removing any pins. Tie the drawstrings firmly, cutting the ends.
For added strength, hammer ½in (1cm) upholstery tacks at regular intervals around the footstool.

7. Screw the pad back onto its base.

8. If desired, edge with flat braid using a curved needle. Stand back and admire!

TRINKET BOX AND GLASSES CASE
(pp 78–81)

The design for the trinket box may be attached in much the same way as the pincushion design described earlier, or you may prefer to lace it on as described on page 125. Either way is suitable.

The glasses case is quite simple to make, follow the instructions 1–7.

1. Decide which end of the design is to be the opening. Pin and tack (baste) it to the backing material, right sides together.

2. Remove pins and sew along three sides only.

3. Trim surplus canvas to within ½in (1cm) of sewing. Neaten raw edges. Turn right side out. Fold under surplus material at the opening, and pin in place.

4. Fold cotton lining material in half. Pin, tack and sew along two sides 1in (2.5cm) from edge leaving one short side open. Trim to within ½in (1cm) of sewing.

5. Turn down the opening until lining is same size as the case.

6. Insert lining into case, wrong sides together. Pin and neatly sew around the opening.

7. Edge with braid to complete.

WAISTCOAT
(pp 72–3)

The waistcoat with the cat and dog face design is for a teddy bear, but could be adapted to fit either a child or an adult. Keep the basic design and work on the same mesh canvas, using a dressmaking pattern to create the desired size and shape.

1. Pin waistcoat panels to lining fabric, right sides together. Tack (baste) and remove pins. Join all edges except the sides under the armholes.

2. Trim to within ¼in (0.5cm) of the stitching and notch around the curve of the armholes. Neaten raw edges. Turn right side out.

3. Cut the fabric for the back to desired shape. The bear in the project has a humpback, so I made a paper pattern to fit. The back should be slightly wider than the two panels. Make a neat hem all the way around except for the sides under the armholes.

4. Match the sides of each panel to the back of the waistcoat and sew neat seams.

5. Fit the garment on the bear. If the back appears loose, make two pleats at the waist, stitch in place and add decorative buttons and a chain for effect.

AFTERCARE

Your finished needlework should last for years to come. Framed pictures can be protected from dust by placing them behind glass. Keep them out of direct sunlight, and sign and date the back.

Cushions and other pieces should never be washed. Accidental stains can be gently dabbed with soap and warm water. Pat dry but never rub. Upholstery such as footstools will benefit from being cleaned occasionally with a vacuum.

SUPPLIERS

Coats Patons Crafts (Anchor)
PO Box
McMullen Road
Darlington
Co. Durham DL1 1YQ
Tel: 01325 381010

DMC Creative World Ltd
Pullman Road
Wigston
Leicestershire LE18 2DY
Tel: 0116 2811040

The DMC Corporation
Port Kearny
Building 10
South Kearny
New Jersey 07032
USA
Tel: 201 589 0606/8931

Joan Toggit Ltd (Zweigart)
2 Riverview Drive
Somerset
New Jersey 08873
USA
Tel: 908 271 1949/0758

The following specialist suppliers welcome all enquiries and orders (including overseas) if you mention this publication.

Clock House Furniture
(Footstools, pp50, 82)
The Old Stables
Overhailes
Haddington
East Lothian
Scotland EH41 3SB
Tel: 01620 860 968

"Remember When"
(Finishing products, pp62, 70, 78)
Cheriton Cottage
Wreningham
Norwich NR16 1BE
Tel: 01508 489 694

Tollit and Harvey Ltd
(Graph paper)
Charts and Art Materials Division
Lyon Way
Greenford
Middlesex UB6 0BN
Tel: 0181 578 6861

ACKNOWLEDGEMENTS

Firstly I would like to thank Vivienne Wells for her constant encouragement. Also, Brenda Morrison and Sue Rhodes at David & Charles for all their hard work. To Maggi McCormick for her helpful editing and invaluable advice. To Cara Ackerman at DMC Creative World for keeping me constantly supplied with yarns and canvas, Julie Gill at Coats Patons Crafts (Anchor wools), and Bill Brown at Tollit and Harvey Ltd (graph paper).

My special thanks to Nicholas Parry at Clock House Furniture for the splendid footstools and Ian Foster at "Remember When" for the round footstool and the other quality needlework products. Also to David Johnson for his splendid photography.

A big hug to Harry Field for making the Penny Farthing Clock frame and to Andrew Field for typing my manuscript and learning to thread a needle to help me complete the remaining projects on time.

INDEX

aftercare, 126
Aida fabric, 114
antique canvas, 114
Art Deco, 82

backing fabric, 123
    moiré, 72
back stitch, 124
Bargello stitch, 122
basting stitch, 124
Berlin woolwork, 46
Black Cat, 100–1
blanket stitch, 124
blocking (stretching), 115
braids & cords, 123, 125
brick stitch, 122
Buccaneer Cat, 66–9
buttonhole stitch, 124

canvas, 114
Cat with Flowers, 108–11
charts, how to use, 8
chequer stitch, 121
clock design, 74–7, 125–6
collie dog, 74–7, 96–9
colour
    of canvas, 114
    of yarns/threads, 117
continental stitch, 118
cords & braids, 123, 125
cotton materials, 123
cotton threads, 95, 114
crewel wool, 113
crewelwork, 78
cushions, making up, 124–5

daschund dog, 96–9
design aspects, 116–17
diagonal stitch, 122
distortion of needlework, 115
dog roses, 46–7
Dogs in the Park, 96–9
double canvas, 114

enlarging designs, 116
equipment, 115
    suppliers, 127

fabrics
    canvas, 114
    for finishing projects, 123
faces, cat & dog, 70–3
fan stitch, 121
finishing projects, 123–6
Florentine stitch, 122
floss, 114
flowers, 22, 46–9, 62–5
footstools, 50–5, 62–5, 126

frames & framing
    mounting & framing, 125
    tapestry frames, 115
fraying, 114, 124
free stitch, 119
French knot, 121

Gallé Cats, 10–19, 125
Gallé, Emile, 12
gathering stitch, 124, 126
ginger cats, 90
    Ginger Cat, 104–5
glasses case, 78–80, 126
gobelin stitches, 120
Grey Cat, 102–3
greyhound, 22, 35
gros point, 118

half-cross stitch, 118
hem stitch, 124
hunting dogs, 78–81, 96–9

interlock canvas, 114

kittens, 37–9
    Kittens with Flowers, 45–9

labrador dog, 96–9
lacing pictures onto board, 125
leaf stitch, 119
lilies, 46–7
lining materials, 123
long and short stitch, 119

making-up projects, 123–6
marking pen, 115
materials, 113–14, 123–4
    suppliers, 127
Maurice and Lulu, 89–93
Medieval Running Dogs, 78–81
moiré backing fabric, 72
mono canvas, 114
mounting, see frames & framing
mouse, 104–5

needles, 115

old English sheepdog, 96–9
overcast stitch, 124

Penelope canvas, 114
Penny Farthing Clock, 74–7,
    125–6
perlé mercerised cotton, 114
Persian yarn, 114
petit point, 118
pincushion, 70–3, 126
pointer dog, 50–5, 82–7

puppies, 22, 37–41

random long stitch, 122
Reclining Cat, 62–5
retriever dog, 96–9
roses, 48–9, 62–5
rugs, 62, 104–5

St Bernard dog, 96–9
samplers, 46, 95
satin stitch, 121
setting (stretching), 115
sheepdog, 96–9
Siamese Cat, 106–7
single canvas, 114
slip stitch, 124
spectacles case, 78–80, 126
Staffordshire Dogs, 21–35, 125
stain removal, 126
starch, 115
stitches, 118–22
    creative, 95–111
    finishing projects, 124
straight stitch, 119
stranded cotton, 114
stretching, 115
Stubbs Dog, 50–5
Stubbs, George, 50
suppliers, 127

tabby cats, 42–3, 46–8, 66–9,
    88–90, 92–3
tacking stitch, 124
tartan plaid, 72
tassels, 123, 125
techniques, 115, 124
    see also stitches
tension of stitches, 115
tent stitch, 118
terrier dog, 96–9
threads, 113–14
Three-Legged Race, 57–61
tortoiseshell cat, 62–5
trinket box, 78–9, 81, 126

uneven stitching, 115

Victorians, 38, 46, 58, 100

waistcoat, 72–3, 126
Walking the Dog, 82–7
Wedding cushion, 58, 60–1
wools, tapestry, 113

yarns, 113–14, 117

zig-zag stitching, 122, 124
zip fastening, 123–5